Using Differ Classroom Assessment to Enhance Student Learning

Using Differentiated Classroom Assessment to Enhance Student Learning introduces pre- and in-service teachers to the foundations, data use, and best practices of the DCA framework. As differentiated instruction practices increasingly enable K-12 educators to individualize learning in their classrooms, it is important that this framework be extended to assessment as well. This concise yet comprehensive book explains the science and rationale behind DCA as well as principles and strategies for both formative and summative assessments. Replete with vignettes, sample outputs, and recommendations, this is a lively and much-needed guide to understanding, enacting, and analyzing grouped and individualized assessments.

Tonya R. Moon is Professor of Curriculum, Instruction, and Special Education in the Curry School of Education at the University of Virginia, USA.

Catherine M. Brighton is Associate Dean of Academic Programs and Student Affairs and Professor of Curriculum, Instruction, and Special Education in the Curry School of Education at the University of Virginia, USA.

Carol A. Tomlinson is former Department Chair and William Clay Parrish, Jr. Professor Emeritus of Leadership, Foundations, and Policy in the Curry School of Education at the University of Virginia, USA.

Student Assessment for Educators
Edited by James H. McMillan,
Virginia Commonwealth University, USA

Using Students' Assessment Mistakes and Learning
Deficits to Enhance Motivation and Learning
James H. McMillan

Using Feedback to Improve Learning
Maria Araceli Ruiz-Primo and Susan M. Brookhart

Using Self-Assessment to Improve Student Learning
Lois Ruth Harris and Gavin T. L. Brown

Using Peer Assessment to Inspire Reflection and Learning
Keith J. Topping

Using Formative Assessment to Support Student
Learning Objectives
M. Christina Schneider and Robert L. Johnson

Managing Classroom Assessment to Enhance
Student Learning
Nicole Barnes and Helenrose Fives

Using Differentiated Classroom Assessment
to Enhance Student Learning
*Tonya R. Moon, Catherine M. Brighton,
and Carol A. Tomlinson*

For more information about this series, please visit: https://
www.routledge.com/Student-Assessment-for-Educators/
book-series/SAFE

Using Differentiated Classroom Assessment to Enhance Student Learning

Tonya R. Moon,
Catherine M. Brighton,
and Carol A. Tomlinson

Routledge
Taylor & Francis Group

NEW YORK AND LONDON

First published 2020
by Routledge
52 Vanderbilt Avenue, New York, NY 10017

and by Routledge
2 Park Square, Milton Park, Abingdon, Oxon, OX14 4RN

Routledge is an imprint of the Taylor & Francis Group, an informa business

Library of Congress Cataloging-in-Publication Data
A catalog record for this title has been requested

ISBN: 978-1-138-32096-3 (hbk)
ISBN: 978-1-138-32097-0 (pbk)
ISBN: 978-0-429-45299-4 (ebk)

Typeset in Sabon
by codeMantra

Contents

About the Authors

Catherine M. Brighton, Ph.D., is Associate Dean for Academic Programs & Student Services and Professor of Curriculum & Instruction in the Curry School of Education and Human Development, University of Virginia, where she also serves as the Co-Director of the University of Virginia Institutes on Academic Diversity. Catherine's research interests include teacher change and school reform initiatives, differentiating curriculum, instruction, and assessment, and qualitative methodologies. She is currently Co-Principal Investigator on a US Department of Education-funded grant on talent development through the lens of literacy. Catherine also led a multi-year project for the National Research Center on the Gifted & Talented focus on differentiating instruction in middle-grade classrooms with diverse student populations.

Tonya R. Moon, Ph.D., is on the faculty at the University of Virginia, Curry School of Education and Human Development where she is a Professor in the Department of Curriculum, Instruction, and Special Education, and Co-Director of the University of Virginia Institutes on Academic Diversity. In addition to her research and teaching responsibilities, she also serves as the University's Chair of the Institutional Review Board for the Social and Behavior Sciences, the body at the university that is charged with reviewing human subjects research. Her research interests include the use of student data for supporting students' academic needs. She works with educators nationally and internationally in the area of assessment to better address the academic diversity of today's classrooms.

Carol A. Tomlinson, Ed.D., is William Clay Parrish, Jr. Professor Emeritus at the University of Virginia's Curry School of Education where she served as Chair of Educational Leadership, Foundations, and Policy, and Co-Director of the University's Institutes on Academic Diversity. Prior to joining the faculty at UVa, she was a public school teacher for 21 years. She was Virginia's Teacher of the Year in 1974. At UVa, she was named Outstanding Professor in 2004 and received an All-University Teaching Award in 2008. In 2019, she was ranked #8 in the *Education Week* Edu-Scholar Public Presence Rankings of 200 "University-based academics who are contributing most substantially to public debates about schools and schooling," and as the #3 voice in Educational Psychology. Her books on differentiation have been translated into 14 languages. Among those books is *Assessment in a Differentiated Classroom: A Guide for Student Success*, which she co-authored with Tonya R. Moon.

1

Why Differentiated Classroom Assessment? Why Now?

Consider these classroom scenarios:

1. Miss Apple works with and designs lessons for 30 or more students who differ in age, ranging from 5 to 17 (grades 1–8) but who otherwise are very similar in terms of race, ethnicity, and English language proficiency. Rather than organizing the students by grade level, she identifies the needs of students in specific areas (reading, writing, arithmetic, history, and geography) and they work together to learn and complete necessary tasks. In front of the teacher's desk is a bench where groups of students are called to read aloud to the teacher or solve specific problems to evidence their developing understandings. From this, she noted students' progress.

2. Mr. Barnes is assigned to work with groups of students organized into grade levels by age, and the lessons are characterized by lectures delivered to the entire group at once.

Most students share common racial and cultural backgrounds, although there are some recent immigrants who have joined the class. Students complete examinations to demonstrate their progress with the expectation that all students will move together to the next grade-level assignment upon completion of the year's lessons.

3. Ms. Conner teaches fifth grade in a class of 25 students ranging from 9 to 11 years old. The class is diverse with students identifying as Caucasian, African American, Latinx, and multi-racial. Several students who are English Language Learners (ELLs) receive English as Second Language (ESL) services, and others have designated support needs noted in 504 Plans and individual education plans (IEPs). One student has a documented physical disability that can present challenges in certain classroom activities. Several students participate in the federal free and reduced lunch program. The 25 students not only vary in terms of cultural and language characteristics, but also in terms of their interests both within and outside of school, their readiness to learn, as well as their individual preferences for interacting with academic materials. Ms. Conner's principal expects her to use data to inform her classroom instruction in ways that acknowledge, value, and support students with a broad array of learning preferences and needs.

The descriptions of the classrooms above provide a brief glimpse into the shifting characteristics of American education. The first, from a one-room schoolhouse, embodies a multi-age, multi-level classroom where addressing student variance was a given and the teacher planned instruction based on students' current points of entry into a topic or skill-set. Students collaborated in a variety of teacher-guided learning groups designed to help all students progress from their current points of development while the teacher instructed individuals and small groups of students with the same goal in mind. Assessment at the recitation bench was an organic part of Miss Apple's classroom, helping her determine when students were ready to progress to the next set of skills and topics. In this classroom, and others like it across the

United States, there was no illusion that students of the same age would fare well by doing the same work, at the same time, with the same support. What we now call differentiation was simply how teachers planned and how students learned.

The second scenario is typical of 19th-century American classrooms, and it reflects the influence of America's rapidly changing economy, the shift from agriculture to industry, and an increasing number of immigrants joining the new workforce. Schools were changing to prepare young people for the new world of work they would enter and to which they would need to contribute. Perceived efficiency was the order of the day, and classrooms now contained students of the same age. The assumption was that all six-year olds, for example, could successfully pursue learning in a lockstep progression. Also during this time, single examinations determined whether students progressed to the next grade level, and there was scant, if any, provision for students who were outliers. In many ways, schools mirrored the factories for which their students were being prepared.

The third scenario reflects typical classrooms across the United States today. An obvious marker of today's classroom is the rise of diversity in many forms. School systems around the nation are experiencing rapid growth in the number of culturally and linguistically diverse students, while about 13% of school-age students receive special education services (https://nces.ed.gov/programs/coe/indicator_cgg.asp) for identified exceptionalities. About 6% of students are identified as academically gifted (https://www.nea.org/assets/docs/twiceexceptional.pdf); about 1 in 59 students are identified with autism spectrum disorder (ASD; https://www.cdc.gov/ncbddd/autism/data.html); and parents' reports of approximately 64% of children aged 2–17 having a mental, emotional, or behavioral disorder at some point during their school careers (https://www.cdc.gov/ncbddd/autism/data.html). Some students, of course, have learning issues that cross multiple categories and may be English language learners as well. Further, there are students who come to school from both privileged and economically disadvantaged environments, and they manifest diversity in less evident ways as well (for example, different levels of motivation to do school, varied world views, a great range of personal interests). It is also the case that students come to the classroom with a wide array of experiences, both inside and outside of school, a variety of ways in which they approach learning, and varying social identities. All of these sources of learner variance, of course, have considerable bearing on learning success. This sweeping range of diversity, perhaps more than any other characteristic, defines 21st-century classrooms. Challenging as it is to effectively teach each learner in classrooms typified by such a degree of diversity, these classrooms also provide a considerable opportunity to prepare young people for life in a 21st-century world in which the ability to appreciate and work harmoniously and productively with people from many different cultures and exceptionalities whose perspectives, proclivities, and talents are sculpted, at least in part, by those exceptionalities and cultures.

The challenge of teaching in academically diverse classrooms is amplified by the nearly two-decade, single-minded emphasis on high-stakes testing—a second core reality in U.S. public school classrooms. A baseline assumption of high-stakes testing is that all students should be ready to succeed on the prescribed tests at the same time in the school year, with accommodations available only in documented need instances. Building administrators and teachers are held accountable for student outcomes on the tests, without regard to student language, economic status, adult support, and life experiences—and sometimes even without regard to learner exceptionality. The resulting pressure to prepare all students to master an over-abundance of content by a specified date causes many teachers to feel they have no choice but to steamroll through their curricula so they will have "covered" massive amounts of rigid and prescriptive content prior to the test date. This inclination is reinforced and amplified by pacing guides and/or required lesson plans that must be carried out in a specific sequence according to a rigid timeline.

This kind of accountability policy is paradoxical in at least two ways. First, it encourages teachers largely to ignore the student variance they continually observe in their classes, and results in one-size-fits-all instruction at the very point in our history when individual student-focused instruction is most needed. Second, the policies that were intended to yield primary benefit for students from low-income and minority groups appear to serve these students particularly poorly (though the policies appear to serve few students well). Since the implementation of high-stakes accountability testing in public schools was mandated by *No Child Left Behind* (2001), a great deal was documented about the unintended consequences of such legislation. Although the law's intent was to reduce on-going achievement gaps, there exists little to no evidence that there has been any closing of the gaps (Nichols & Harris, 2016). Rather, evidence of high-stakes testing practices indicates that teachers' instructional and assessment practices follow a narrow curriculum where students are not exposed to non-tested content and, instead, engage in a steady diet of test preparation activities (e.g., Herman, 2004; Koretz, 2017; Moon, Brighton, & Callahan, 2003; Moon, Callahan, & Tomlinson, 2003).

While the testing accountability policies' intent is to increase student learning, according to recent government reports (https://www.nationsreportcard.gov/), only about one-third of U.S. fourth- and eighth-grade students read at a proficient level as measured by the National Assessment of Educational Progress (NAEP). Many scholars and policymakers point to the combination of demographic shifts in U.S. classrooms and annual testing policies as root causes of the stagnation. For students leaving the K-12 educational system, national rates of remediation in post-secondary institutions indicate that many students are underprepared to engage in college-level work, with 40%–60% of students entering the first year requiring remediation in English, mathematics, or both (http://www.highereducation.org/reports/college_readiness/CollegeReadiness.pdf). The problem is more acute for low-income students and students of color, with 56% of African American students and 45% of Latinx students enrolling in remedial post-secondary courses nationwide, compared to 35% of white students. The renewed emphasis on accountability policies found in the *Every Student Succeeds Act* (ESSA, 2015) does little to lessen teachers' conclusion that "one-size-fits-all" teaching and assessment is their only instructional option.

Re-creating the Classroom: A Different Approach to Instruction and Assessment

Excellent teaching is both an art and a science. Our two-decade-long experiment with achievement via test-driven pedagogy, rigid, often de-contextualized and low-relevance curriculum, and classrooms in which young human beings take a back seat to test scores, is clearly anything but artful. That approach is also inconsistent with our best knowledge about the science of teaching—as we will see in Chapter 2. Further, we have ample evidence that in one-size-fits-all classrooms few, if any, students have their needs met.

Differentiated instruction (Sousa & Tomlinson, 2018; Tomlinson, 2014, 2017; Tomlinson & Imbeau, 2010; Tomlinson & Moon, 2013) provides a framework for re-designing classrooms to place individual students in the center of learning, uses curriculum that enlivens learning, provides instruction that reflects both the art and science of teaching, and creates learning environments that enhance the development of both students and teachers. Central to Tomlinson's (2001) original model of differentiation is the role of formative/on-going assessment as a vehicle for advancing learning. In this book, we will expand the original model to include focusing on the critical role of differentiated assessment, including both formative and summative, in understanding students' varied learning needs, guiding instructional planning, and developing student agency in learning.

Before we begin exploring the purpose, practice, and promise of assessment in differentiated classrooms, it is helpful to provide a brief overview of the broader model of differentiation. The purpose here is not to explore the model in depth, but rather to establish the context in which we envision assessment—and to provide readers with a "refresher" on the model.

Differentiation

Differentiation is rooted in a philosophy that is guided by five principles, and enacted through the use of several key practices.

All of these aspects inform and shape the nature and use of assessment in differentiated classrooms. The three tables that follow capture these aspects (Tables 1.1, 1.2, and 1.3).

The philosophy, principles, and practices of differentiation are all "cut from the same cloth"—that is, they stem from the same bodies of research on teaching and learning and work together to create classrooms designed to encourage and support maximum development of the potential of each learner in the classroom—and of the teacher as well. The philosophy, principles, and practices are highly interdependent. For instance, the nature of the learning environment will either encourage or discourage student motivation to learn, which, in turn, will accordingly influence the impact of instruction on student learning. The way in which a teacher envisions and implements assessment practices will make the environment less, or more, invitational for students (Tomlinson & Moon, 2011, 2014). Flat curriculum that has little relevance for learners will necessarily diminish the impact of instruction and the "draw" of the environment,

Table 1.1 Assumptions of Differentiation

Key Assumptions	Brief Explanation of the Assumption
Diversity is normal and valuable.	Inclusion honors the contributions of all individuals. Segregation and isolation are diminishing.
Seeing every student's capacity to learn and contribute is essential to inclusion.	Teachers who believe in both the hidden and evident abilities of their students make room for those abilities to grow in the classroom.
The role of the teacher is to maximize the growth of each learner.	Teachers who accept responsibility for maximizing the growth of each learner plan and teach to realize that goal.
It is the responsibility of schools to ensure that all students consistently have equity of access to excellent learning opportunities.	Teachers and other school leaders have the responsibility to remove barriers that deny many students equal access to excellence.

Table 1.2 Some Key Principles of Differentiation

Principles	Key Indicators of the Principle	Brief Explanation
Quality teaching said learning stem from an invitational learning environment	Teacher with a growth mindset Strong teacher/student connections Strong sense of "team" or "community" in the classroom	Students need to feel safe, valued, appreciated, challenged, and supported in order to learn well
Quality curriculum is foundational to student success	Clear learning targets (KUDs) Emphasis on student understanding Plan for engaging learners	The brain needs "sense" (understanding) and "meaning" (relevance) to learn
Assessment information informs teaching and learning	Strongly aligned with learning targets (KUDs) Emphasizes understanding Used to guide teacher and student planning	Tight alignment of assessment with learning targets focuses assessment appropriately. Information gleaned from assessment is the compass of daily planning
Instruction responds to student variance	Tightly aligned with learning targets (KUDs) Based on assessment information Responsive to student readiness, interest, and approach to learning Proactively planned	Tight alignment of instruction with learning targets focuses teaching and learning effectively. Attention to varied learning needs provides each student with a pathway to grow
Classroom routines should balance flexibility and stability	Students understand and participate in developing a differentiated classroom The teacher leads students and then works with them to manage routines	Developing a differentiated classroom is a team effort that seeks the contributions of everyone in the class to support the success of each learner

Table 1.3 Some Key Practices of Differentiation

The Practice	Description	Rationale
"Teaching up"	Teachers plan first for their advanced students, then differentiate by scaffolding other students to work with the challenging assignments	This approach opens the way for all students to have equity of access to excellent learning opportunities. Differentiate by "teaching up," not by "dumbing down"
Respectful tasks	Every student's work looks equally important, equally appealing, and equally engaging	This respects the dignity of each student and signals the expectation that each student will do meaningful work
Flexible grouping	Students work regularly in a variety of groupings with students who have both similar and different points of readiness, interests, and approaches to learning	This builds community, avoids stereotyping, and extends student awareness of strengths of all members of the class

just as highly engaging curriculum will enliven both instruction and the environment in which it takes place.

Together, the core philosophy, principles, and practices of differentiation guide teachers in effectively differentiating content (what students learn or how they access what they learn), process (how students make sense of and come to "own" the content), products (how students show what they know, understand, and can do), and affect/learning environment (both the physical nature and feelings-related nature of the classroom and interactions in it; Callahan, Moon, Oh, Azano, & Hailey, 2015). Content, process, product, and affect/learning environment are differentiated in response to student readiness (current point of entry into content), interests (student passion for or curiosity about an idea or topic), or learning preferences (ways of engaging with learning at a given time in the learning process). The primary intent of all aspects of differentiation is to facilitate student proficiency with the targets for any segment of learning, and, whenever possible, to guide the learning in moving beyond those targets (Bondie, Dahnka, & Zusho, 2019).

The Role of Assessment in Effective Differentiation

For purposes of this book, six key ideas or components of differentiation will be emphasized:

- The classroom functions as a *Community of Learning* where all students feel safe, supported, respected, and are willing to take the risk of learning.
- *High-Quality Curriculum* engages students with relevant and important knowledge, ideas, and skills that enable them to lead productive and meaningful lives.
- *Respectful Tasks* ensure that work and working conditions for all learners are equally important, equally appealing, and equally engaging, enabling every learner to see him or herself and every other learner as held in high regard by the teacher, expected to do important work, and capable of doing that work. Respectful tasks also take into account student entry point, strengths, interests, and approaches to learning so that success is just within the reach of the learner.
- *Flexible Grouping* allows students to work in a variety of grouping arrangements based on interests, current readiness levels, and/or learning preferences. Groupings are sometimes heterogeneous and sometimes homogeneous in nature and may be selected by students or assigned by the teacher based on the nature of the work and the needs of the learners.
- *Teaching Up* sets a high ceiling of student expectations and scaffolds the process of moving toward those expectations

so that each learner regularly finds the balance of academic challenge and support necessary to extend his or her current levels of proficiency with important content.

• *Continual Assessment* allows teachers to understand students' learning trajectories, both individually and collectively, and to establish and maintain an effectively differentiated classroom. This element is the chief focus of this book. However, it is important to understand that continual, effective differentiated assessment intersects with the other five elements as well.

Building on a foundation of clear and meaningful learning goals, teaching in a differentiated classroom adopts classroom assessment practices that allow you to determine students' progress toward expected milestones and to use current evidence to inform instructional planning. Information derived from differentiated formative assessment guides you in creating purposeful instructional *groupings*, determining the *pace of instruction*, making sound choices about *materials and other resources*, and determining how to *support and extend learning* for students in a given instructional moment. Information derived from differentiated summative assessment guides you in evaluating student learning at the end of an instructional segment whether it be at the end of a series of lessons (e.g., quiz) or at the completion of a unit of study (e.g., performance assessment or exam). In addition, differentiated summative assessments can also be used formatively to guide decisions in subsequent instructional units.

Too often, however, classroom assessment practices follow the one-size-fits-all model, using the same assessments and assessment processes for all students. The resulting data then lead to ill-informed instructional decisions that overlook students' varied learning needs. If the purpose of classroom assessment is to generate insights about students that are as accurate as possible in order to support student-focused decision-making, then using assessment practices that overlook the diversity of students' academic needs suggests a lack of understanding of what constitutes appropriate assessment practice (Marzano, 2000). In classrooms where teachers aspire to reach each student, assessments themselves will often be differentiated to help the teacher understand and address the range of student needs throughout learning cycles as well as increase student agency and involvement in the assessment process.

Classroom Assessments during Formative Assessment

While many definitions exist for formative assessment, the Chief Council of State School Officers (CCSSO, 2008, p. 2), define it as "a planned, ongoing process used by all students and teachers during learning and teaching to elicit and use evidence of student learning to improve student understanding of intended disciplinary learning outcomes and support students to become self-directed learners." Said a bit differently, formative assessment is a process through which a teacher formally or informally collects data on student proficiency with targeted content and analyzes the data to understand patterns of student development in that content, in order to make better decisions about next steps in teaching and learning and to help students plan effectively for continued learning. Appropriate use of formative assessment results in a teacher changing teaching and learning plans with the goal of more positive student outcomes than had the data not been available.

In this book, we will often separate "formative assessment" into two stages—*pre-assessment*, which, as noted above, occurs prior to the start of a unit of study to understand students' points of entry into upcoming unit, and *on-going assessment*, which occurs regularly throughout a unit of study to maintain awareness of students' degrees of progress as the unit unfolds. Both pre- and on-going assessments are types of formative assessment. The distinction simply clarifies the time during which the assessment occurs. We will always use the term pre-assessment to refer to classroom diagnostic assessment that takes place before formal study of a unit begins. We will use the terms formative assessment and on-going assessment interchangeably to refer to assessments that occur throughout a unit of study to inform teaching and learning.

The Differentiated Assessment Cycle: What, When, and Why?

When thinking about differentiated classroom assessment (DCA) and the data that are generated from such assessments, it is helpful to have an understanding of *when* to assess, *what* to assess, and *why* assessment matters. Answering these questions informs the three phases of the assessment cycle within an instructional setting—pre-assessment, on-going/formative assessment, and summative assessment. It is important to note that assessments in any of the three phases can, and often should, be differentiated (Figure 1.1).

Phase I of the Assessment Cycle: Pre-assessment

In effectively differentiated classrooms, teachers gather data at the individual student level prior to the start of a new unit of study or topic because students enter the space with a wide range of pre-existing knowledge, skills, beliefs, attitudes, motivations, and understandings, all of which influence how they will process and integrate new information. This in turn affects how students will think, apply, and create new knowledge, skills, and understandings. Intentionally deciding to gather these data prior to a new unit of study and make sense of the collected data for instructional planning, signals that the teacher intends to align the delivery of instructional content with students'

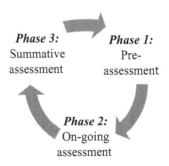

Figure 1.1 Phases of the assessment cycle

needs thereby avoiding pitching the content either beyond or beneath the appropriate place for the students. Pre-assessment data allow you and the student to work with the new content in efficient and productive ways. While teachers often pre-assess student status with upcoming learning targets (KUDs) a day or two before a new unit begins, there is obvious benefit to giving pre-assessments several days before the start of a new unit. Giving pre-assessments several days in advance allows sufficient time in a busy schedule for you to study the pre-assessment result in some depth to identify patterns of student need revealed in the pre-assessment data and to adjust instructional plans accordingly.

Pre-assessments should never be graded. It is important to remember that grades are used to answer the question "How well did a student learn and achieve the identified learning targets?" Grading pre-assessments completely ignores the fact that some students have more knowledge or skills than others before instruction ever begins, thus often penalizing those with less knowledge or skills at the outset. The sole purpose of pre-assessment is to identify where students are relative to identified learning targets prior to instruction in order to know how to target early instruction to learners' varied entry points. You will be most successful in your instructional efforts if all students have at least a basic level of knowledge once the lesson(s) is taught.

Phase II of the Assessment Cycle: On-going Assessment

Fundamental to a differentiated classroom is persistent collection of data to support the teacher's instructional planning and the student's plans for learning as well. This phase of the assessment cycle also supports teacher reflection on the effectiveness of the instructional choices you make in support of student learning to the current point in a unit or sequence of study. Data collected via on-going assessment can be formal or planned assessments (for example, quizzes, exit cards, short answer responses) or informal data (for example, observing student work in process and making notes on the observations, conversations with students about their work, asking students to indicate with a hand signal or colored card their confidence level with an idea or skill). Some of these informal assessments are at the individual student level (e.g., concept map or a student check-in with you). Others are at the whole-class level (e.g., on-the-fly assessment through student finger signals to show degree of mastery).

The importance of the on-going phase of the assessment cycle is that it provides an opportunity for both yourself and your students to focus on what is required next to reach the targeted learning goals. It provides information useful in planning student groupings, differentiating upcoming tasks, and planning next steps for whole class or small group instruction. For the students, on-going assessment provides information about progress to date in a unit and opportunity to regulate or plan for their continued learning. When using on-going assessment information to teach more effectively, the assessment is sometimes referred to as assessment *for* learning, which is not a different idea from formative assessment but rather emphasizes why we do this in our teaching process. When a student uses on-going assessment to better understand their current learning and to plan more proactively for continued growth, the assessment is sometimes referred to as assessment *as* learning. Ideally, many formative (i.e., on-going) assessments serve the dual purpose of assessment *for* and assessment *as* learning (e.g., Earl, 2013). By that, we mean the actual process of engaging with the formative assessment itself serves as a source of learning for the students. Assessment *as* learning places students in the position of self-regulating their own learning through which they make decisions about how they will use feedback in order to move toward mastery of the targeted learning goals. Again, on-going assessments should rarely, if ever, be graded. They take place during the part of the learning cycle when students need practice to master content. When teachers assign grades prematurely during practice, student willingness to continue practicing and risk making mistakes that are necessary for learning diminishes. The goal for formative assessment is providing meaningful, actionable, differentiated feedback that helps a student move forward in learning, not judging or grading students.

Phase III of the Assessment Cycle: Summative Assessment

The third phase of the assessment cycle is summative assessment, sometimes referred to as assessment *of* learning. This phase plays an important role in the instructional planning process because it provides information regarding the degree to which a student has mastered (or exceeded) the pre-determined learning goals (KUDs). Unlike pre- and on-going assessments, summative assessment is generally graded. The summative phase occurs only after students have had the opportunity to engage with and practice the content, allowing sense-making to occur so they are in a good position to demonstrate their level of understanding of the content and skills with some success.

It is important to note that summative assessment can occur both at the end of a series of lessons (i.e., quiz) and at the end of a completed unit of study (e.g., exam). In the former instance, students demonstrate at the end of a discrete segment of learning within a unit of study that they have (or do not have) foundational knowledge upon which subsequent lessons in the unit will build. Examples of this type of summative assessment include short assignments, tests, and quizzes. At the end of a unit, of course, students demonstrate their level of mastery of the larger or complete segment of learning. While both examples are types of summative assessment, those that occur at the end of the unit may be more encompassing (cumulative) than the type that occurs after a series of lessons within the unit. The difference occurs in the level of interpretation and types of decisions that can be made earlier versus later in the summative phase of the cycle. Both types of summative assessment are typically graded. However, the end-of-cycle summative assessment should likely carry more weight in determining reported grades, particularly in instances where the end-of-cycle assessment is cumulative.

This book primarily focuses on how to gather and use data from DCAs (pre-assessments, on-going/formative, summative) to promote learning for all students, with the goal of honoring and serving effectively the full range of academically diverse students in today's classrooms. We also believe it is important to also provide some guidance on how to differentiate classroom assessments themselves. For complete details on this process, you can refer to Tomlinson and Moon (2013).

A (Brief) Guide to Differentiating Classroom Assessment

Inherent in the key practices of differentiation outlined in Table 1.3 is that effective differentiation occurs through one or more mechanisms (Tomlinson, 2017):

1. Differentiation of the content to be taught to different groups of students;
2. Differentiation of the process by which you use different instructional strategies targeted to different groups of students and/or different sense-making strategies that students engage with the content for the purposes of learning; and/or
3. Differentiation of the "product" whereby students demonstrate their learning.

These avenues for differentiation occur in response to learners' interests that may have relevance to the new content to learn, readiness to learn the new content, and/or through the ways in which best set students up for success in learning the content. Undergirding all of this is that the learning goals remain the same (KUDs) regardless of the type of differentiation employed unless noted in special cases (e.g., special education modifications). From a differentiated assessment framework, these same avenues for differentiating the assessment still hold. When the learning targets and the content *remain the same* for all students, the assessment can be differentiated through the ways in which students engage with the assessment content, and/or by the final product students produce in response to assessment requirements. When the learning standards *are not tied to specific content* and thus can be different across students, the assessment's content may be differentiated. For example, in a high school Life Science class, students are studying the interdependence of relationships in ecosystems. One of the learning standards from the Next Generation Science Standards is that students are to test solutions to a proposed problem related to threatened or endangered species (HS-LS4.6, www.nextgenscience.org). In this example, the proposed problem that students tackle may be different (i.e., different content), but the purpose of the assessment remains the same: measuring the HS-LS4.6 standard. The ways that students engage with the assessment task (i.e., process) or the final product may, or may not, be differentiated. It is an important note that not all assessments can or should be differentiated. For example, certain types of assessments (e.g., closed-ended tests—multiple choice, true/false, matching) should only be differentiated by the ways in which students *have access to the assessment* (e.g., paper-and-pencil versus being audio-recorded) or *the way in which they respond* (e.g., paper-and-pencil versus computer or verbally) or the *conditions around their complexity*, such as extended time allowed or completion of the items in a different location. Additional details are provided for consideration of differentiating assessments in upcoming chapters (i.e., Chapters 3 and 4).

The emphasis of the book is on the element of *differentiated assessment* within the context of a differentiated classroom and on how to *interpret* and *use* data that stems from such assessments to make instructional decisions that are appropriate for students' varied academic needs. While instruction is surely a central component of the learning cycle, this text will concentrate primarily on DCA, with emphasis on how data obtained from both formal and informal forms of DCA (formative and summative) help you provide learning experiences that are a good fit for your students.

Figure 1.2 depicts the frequency of administration of classroom assessment relative to the full spectrum of educational assessments given in today's schools. From this figure, it is easy to see that classroom assessments—both formative and summative—are the types of assessments best situated to have a consistent, direct, and positive impact on day-to-day teaching, and therefore on student learning.

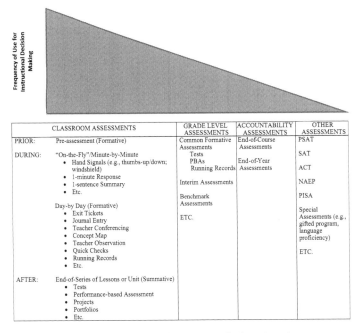

	CLASSROOM ASSESSMENTS	GRADE LEVEL ASSESSMENTS	ACCOUNTABILITY ASSESSMENTS	OTHER ASSESSMENTS
PRIOR:	Pre-assessment (Formative)	Common Formative Assessments	End-of-Course Assessments	PSAT
DURING:	"On-the-Fly"/Minute-by-Minute • Hand Signals (e.g., thumbs-up/down; windshield) • 1-minute Response • 1-sentence Summary • Etc.	Tests PBAs Running Records Interim Assessments Benchmark Assessments ETC.	End-of-Year Assessments	SAT ACT NAEP PISA Special Assessments (e.g., gifted program, language proficiency) ETC.
	Day-by Day (Formative) • Exit Tickets • Journal Entry • Teacher Conferencing • Concept Map • Teacher Observation • Quick Checks • Running Records • Etc.			
AFTER:	End-of-Series of Lessons or Unit (Summative) • Tests • Performance-based Assessment • Projects • Portfolios • Etc.			

Figure 1.2 The continuum and frequency of educational assessments

Four key assumptions undergird this book's focus on DCA:

1. Students differ—they differ in readiness to learn new knowledge and skills, in interests and their ability to engage in the learning process, and in preferences at a given time for taking in, making sense of, and expressing information.
2. Quality teaching requires responding to students' academic needs based on information derived from both formal and informal classroom assessments.
3. Clearly defined learning goals (KUDs) guide effective teaching and establish tight linkages between those curricular goals, assessments, and instruction. Classroom assessment is a crucial resource for ensuring coherence between high-quality curriculum, learning goals embedded in the curriculum, and the process of high-quality teaching.

4. Learning goals:
   a. can be domain-specific (focused on the core ideas and practices of a particular discipline);
   b. can be domain-general (knowledge, understandings, and skills useful across a range of disciplines - e.g. problem-solving, self-regulation, making connections); and
   c. can differ in time span required for student competence—from years (Lehrer & Schauble, 2011) to weeks, days, or even minutes (Siegler, 1995).

These assumptions play out in what Pellegrino, Chudowsky, and Glaser (2001) termed the *Assessment Triangle*, which proposes that there are three areas that underlie all assessment situations—including classroom assessment: *cognition*, *observation*, and *interpretation*. Cognition is the starting point for all teaching and assessment, embodying the core learning targets (knowledge, understandings, skills) on which teachers and students will focus. Observation refers to the methods and analytic tools through which a teacher determines the degree to which students are meeting the intended learning targets. Finally, interpretation represents the process of eliciting evidence from the assessments to inform instructional decisions. The premise is represented by an inverted triangle where the base represents the cognition component, which highlights the importance of having clarity about learning targets. In instances where there is a misalignment between the KUDs and the methods and analytic tools used to assess intended learning targets, the resulting data are not useful for making instructional inferences about students' learning. If, however, the KUDs are too narrow or broad, then the methods employed to gather evidence of student learning do not lend themselves to differentiation. In either case, high-quality data are not obtained, which results in teachers making ill-informed instructional decisions.

We will focus on applying this conceptual framework to the process of facilitating learning based on DCA and data resulting from such assessment.

Looking Back and Ahead

This chapter highlights the current diversity of today's classrooms and the inevitability of diversity in classrooms for the foreseeable future. It provides a digest of the elements of differentiation from which the practice of DCA derives. It also establishes a case for using classroom assessment data to enhance student learning in differentiated classrooms.

In the next chapter, we provide a digest of theoretical and empirical literatures that frame the model for DCA. There is strong scientific evidence for DCA and for using data from these assessments to better position students for mastering essential learning goals.

Chapter 3 examines the role of pre- and on-going assessment data in instructional planning and how to make sense of that formative assessment evidence in a way that leads teachers to make meaningful decisions. Chapter 4 parallels Chapter 3 by looking at the same questions as Chapter 3, but in regard to summative rather than formative assessment data. Chapter 4 places particular emphasis on differentiated performance assessments.

The final chapter brings the ideas explored in the earlier chapters together by providing a process for using data from DCA to plan instruction. It provides readers with recommendations and useful tips to inform data-use work in this aspect of successful teaching. We hope you will find the ideas accessible, the tools practical, and the "cases in point" relatable.

References

Bondie, R. S., Dahnka, C., & Zusho, A. (2019). How does changing "one-size-fits-all" to differentiated instruction affect teaching? *Review of Educational Research, 43*, 336–362. doi: 10.3102/0091732X18821120.

Callahan, C. M., Moon, T. R., Oh, S., Azano, A. P., & Hailey, E. P. (2015). What works in gifted education: Documenting effects of an integrated curricular/instructional model. *American Educational Research Journal, 52*, 1–31. doi: 10.3102/0002831214549448.

Council of Chief State School Officers. (2008). *Revising the definition of formative assessment*. Author.

Earl, L. (2013). *Assessment as learning: Using classroom assessment to maximize student learning*. Thousand Oaks, CA: Corwin.

Every Child Succeeds Act (ESSA) of 2015, Public Law No. 114–195, S.1177, 114th Cong. (2015). Retrieved from https://www.congress.gov/114/plaws/publ95/PLAW-114publ95.pdf.

Herman, J. L. (2004). The effects of testing on instruction. In S. H. Fuhrman & R. F. Elmore (Eds.). *Redesigning accountability systems for education* (pp. 141–166). New York, NY: Teachers College Press.

Koretz, D. (2017). *The testing charade: Pretending to make schools better*. Chicago, IL: University of Chicago Press.

Lehrer, R., & Schauble, L. (2011). Designing to support long-term growth and development. In T. Koschmann (Ed.), *Theories of learning and studies of instructional practice* (pp. 19–38). New York, NY: Springer.

Marzano, R. (2000). *Transforming classroom grading*. Alexandria, VA: ASCD.

Moon, T. R., Brighton, C. M., & Callahan, C. M. (2003). The influences of state testing programs on elementary teachers and students. *The Roeper Review, 25*(2), 49–60.

Moon, T. R., Callahan, C.M., & Tomlinson, C.A. (2003). Effects of state testing programs on elementary schools with high concentrations of student poverty – Good news or bad news? *Current Issues in Education* [On-line], *6*(8). Retrieved from https://cie.asu.edu/ojs/index.php/cieatasu/article/view/1683.

Nichols, S. L., & Harris, L. R. (2016). Accountability assessment's effects on teachers and schools. In G. T. L. Brown & L. R. Harris (Eds.), *Handbook of human and social conditions in assessment* (pp. 40–56). New York, NY: Routledge. doi: 10.4324/9781315749136.ch3

Pellegrino, J. W., Chudowsky, N., & Glaser, R. (2001). *Knowing what students know: The science and design of educational assessment*. Committee on the Foundations of Assessment, Board on Testing and Assessment, Center for Education, National Research Council. Washington, DC: National Academies Press.

Siegler, R. S. (1995). How does change occur: A microgenetic study of number conservation. *Cognitive Psychology, 25*, 225–273.

Sousa, D., & Tomlinson, C. (2018). *Differentiation and the brain: How neuroscience supports the learner-friendly classroom* (2nd Ed.). Bloomington, IN: Solution Tree.

Tomlinson, C. (2001). *How to differentiate instruction in mixed-ability classrooms* (2nd Ed.). Alexandria, VA: ASCD.

Tomlinson, C. (2014). *The differentiated classroom: Responding to the needs of all learners* (2nd Ed.). Alexandria, VA: ASCD.

Tomlinson, C. (2017). *How to differentiate instruction in academically diverse classrooms* (3rd Ed.). Alexandria, VA: ASCD.

Tomlinson, C., & Imbeau, M. (2010). *Leading and managing a differentiated classroom.* Alexandria, VA: ASCD.

Tomlinson, C. A., & Moon, T. R. (2011). The relationship between assessment and differentiation. *Better: Evidence-Based Education, 3*(3), 3–4.

Tomlinson, C. A., & Moon, T. R. (2013). *Assessment and student success in a differentiated classroom.* Alexandria, VA: ASCD.

Tomlinson, C. A., & Moon, T. R. (2014). The relationship between assessment and differentiation. In R. E. Slavin (Ed.), *Proven practices in education: Classroom management and assessment* (pp. 1–5). Thousand Oaks, CA: Corwin.

2

The Science behind Differentiated Classroom Assessment

For centuries, beliefs about student learning were based on the premise that a person was born with "tabula rasa"—a blank slate that would be written upon by experiences and perceptions, or a mind like an empty vessel waiting to be filled with information. While we still see evidence of those ancient philosophies in the ways we "do school," we now have a better sense of how the brain is structured at birth, and how those structures support learning. We know, for example, that the brain is organized at birth to help humans make meaning of the world around them, to learn from social interaction (Darling-Hammond, Flook, Cook-Harvey, Barron, & Osher, 2019), and to arrange and store information in ways that support meaning and efficient retrieval of that information (e.g., Lenroot & Giedd, 2007). We have evidence from research in psychology and neuroscience that the process of learning involves complex interactions (Zelazo, Blair, & Willoughby, 2017), such as reconciling new information with prior knowledge (Darling-Hammond, et al., 2019), monitoring the physical and social context where learning may occur, and cultivating positive relationships among the teacher, student, peers, and new content. It is helpful as we explore the principles and practices of differentiated assessment to briefly examine five research-supported pillars that have direct relevance to those principles and practices.

- Growth mindset is foundational to the nature and purpose of assessment;
- New knowledge builds on and extends a learner's prior knowledge and experiences;
- People learn when challenges are in their Zone of Proximal Development (ZPD)—when the challenges are a bit beyond their reach and they have the support necessary to extend their reach;
- Learning progressions provide a roadmap for assessment and instructional planning based on information gleaned from that assessment; and
- A social classroom environment supports learning through co-construction of knowledge, understanding, and skills.

Growth Mindset as Foundation for Differentiated Classroom Assessment

Consider the following scenario:

Seventh-grade students Carlos and Tomas share the same physical education class. As part of the curriculum called Active Bodies-Healthy Lives, students complete short mini-courses, each focused on a different sporting activity and its benefits for healthy living. The current session is focused on golfing. During each class, local golf enthusiasts guide students as they learn new golf techniques. Following each lesson, students practice the new skill. During the last week of the course, Mr. Jones, the golf pro from a local recreation league, watches each of the students swing the clubs and drive balls into the field so he can provide feedback to help each student improve their skills.

Later, the boys discussed the last golf session as they changed classes.

Carlos—I learned so much from Mr. Jones! I never thought about golf before this class but now I'm excited to keep practicing my swing and all the things we talked about.

Tomas—Not me! All he ever told me was what I did wrong. I stink at golf, and I'll never play again!

All classroom exchanges communicate tacit beliefs and assumptions, but perhaps none more powerfully than the messages we communicate through the ways we handle assessments, the ways we interpret success or failure based on assessments, the decisions we make as a result of students' performances on assessments, and how we share information from assessments with learners and other relevant stakeholders. In teaching, it is easy over time to forget the power assessments hold in students' minds (McMillan, 2016). McMillan's review of the literature on student perceptions regarding assessment suggests that there are factors that affect students' performances and their reactions to their performances prior to an assessment event, during an assessment event, and after an assessment event. Understanding these factors and their implications for teaching is an important aspect of student learning. What we might consider to be a minor exchange about a student's progress sends messages to those students about themselves as learners and our beliefs about the likelihood that they can be successful in their endeavors well beyond the sphere of the assessment. In the end, our assessment practices influence students' beliefs about learning, their purpose as learners, and even their worth as human beings. Therefore, it is helpful to start our discussion of the science of learning with the importance of expectations and motivation as those elements relate to assessment.

Assessments should be tools for educators and students to gauge a student's progress toward developing expertise in a given area. Assessments should serve as a source of student and teacher reflection that motivates both of them to persist. However, assessments often become obstacles rather than springboards to success when students equate struggle with lack of capacity, and interpret assessment results that show opportunities for growth to be tantamount to failure. In the example of golf class, Carlos approached the feedback he received as guidance that enabled him to continue improving his skills. In contrast, Tomas interpreted the feedback he received as an indictment of poor performance and inadequate ability. Through that lens, his decision to walk away from the sport entirely seemed the best way to avoid further discomfort and erosion of self-concept. At this point, Carlos reflected a "growth mindset" and Tomas a "fixed mindset." Teachers who want to ensure that their students grow as learners and see learning as key to building promising lives understand the importance of helping each learner develop a growth mindset. Because of the weight educators and schools place on measuring student growth, the way a teacher thinks about, uses, and communicates to students about assessment will likely be instrumental in shaping a student's mindset in ways that will undergird or undercut learning for a considerable period of time.

The psychological theory of mindset has emerged over the past three decades (for example, Dweck, 2006). It proposes intrinsic theories of intelligence, or mindsets, along a continuum from *fixed* (ability is in-born and cannot be markedly changed) to *growth* (ability can be developed throughout life). Psychologists David Yeager and Carol Dweck define mindset as "core assumptions about the malleability of personal qualities" (Yeager & Dweck, 2012, p. 303). A large body of research across a variety of settings and conditions indicates that academic mindsets can be quite influential in student motivation to learn, as well as in learning itself. A growth mindset can increase student motivation (e.g., Ng, 2018), contribute to student sense of belonging in an academic setting (e.g., Rattan, Good, & Dweck, 2012; Walton & Cohen, 2011), reduce achievement gaps across racial, social class, and gender groups (e.g., Blackwell, Trzensniewski, & Dweck, 2007; Claro, Paunesku, & Dweck, 2016; Degol, Wang, Zhang, & Allerton, 2018; Walton & Cohen, 2011), and build resilience in the face of difficulty (Blackwell et al., 2007). Research findings on mindset indicate that mindset can be shaped by expectations of self and others (e.g., Siegle, McCoach, &

Roberts, 2017), through feedback (Smith, Brumskill, Johnson, & Zimmer, 2018), and through explicit teaching about mindset (Aronson, Fried, & Good, 2002).

Within educational settings, mindset manifests in goal orientations that greatly impact a student's approach to learning and learning outcomes. Students who have a *learning goal orientation* believe that mastery develops over time with practice and persistence. These students tend to find learning both challenging and satisfying and therefore learn for the sake of learning. By contrast, students with a *performance goal orientation* believe their abilities come from innate talent and that practice and persistence cannot significantly change that reality. Rather than valuing learning for its own sake, these students generally learn for the sake of rewards—or to avoid some sort of punishment. Too often schools further reinforce this performance-focused orientation. In the golf example, Carlos exhibited a learning goal orientation while Tomas evidenced a performance goal orientation. Students who learn because learning is satisfying are much more likely to continue to pursue learning over a lifetime than are students with performance orientations. Individuals who are motivated by rewards most often lose their motivation to learn when the rewards cease.

Mindset theory is especially important to consider in the context of differentiated assessment because in order to optimize students' academic achievement, both teachers and students must view the process of assessing, providing feedback, and responding productively to feedback as opportunities to learn and to enhance deeper understanding and skills. In other words, assessment must be envisioned, implemented, and presented in ways that reinforce a growth mindset, a learning orientation, for both students and teachers. It is important that both teachers and students view the opportunity to gather and act on information about progress toward learning goals as key to student success. When differentiated classroom assessment is implemented by a teacher with a growth mindset, with the intent to help students develop a growth mindset, it increases the chances that a student's experience with the assessment is an encouragement—an invitation to learn—rather than causing the student to feel discouraged about the likelihood that his or her participation in learning will lead to growth and success. Differentiated classroom assessment should be an invitation to students to be partners in and ultimately agents of their own learning. Likewise, teachers who approach differentiated assessment with a growth mindset are more likely to develop a deeper belief in the capacity of each student to succeed, and to develop a greater sense of their own agency as a teacher, as they come to understand the positive impact of assessment-informed instructional planning on the growth of their academically diverse students.

Building on Prior Knowledge to Gain New Knowledge

A second key principle to guide a consideration of differentiated classroom assessment is the importance of building upon students' prior knowledge. Phases I and II of the assessment cycle discussed in Chapter 1 outline not only the rationale for building on prior knowledge but also offer suggestions on how to build on students' prior knowledge. Each student comes to a classroom with educational and personal experiences that shape how they respond to teaching and learning—and, in fact, each student likely brings different constellations of backgrounds and perspectives. Students' brains are active seekers and processors of information. They attend to environmental elements (e.g., the teacher's mood, peers, instruction), encode the information to be learned, relate the new information to knowledge already in memory, store the new knowledge in memory, and retrieve it as needed (Schunk, 2016). From an instructional perspective, this provides support for differentiated instruction and assessment because with differentiation, both instruction and assessment are designed to build upon a student's prior knowledge and to enable each student to make connections between what she/he already knows and what she/he is about to learn.

Given that students come to classrooms all along the continuum of experiences, knowledge, and skills, and presuming that instruction is built around these differences (i.e., differentiated instruction), the same rationale applies to using differentiated classroom assessments. That is, by gathering data about students' knowledge, understandings, and skills related to a new topic of study through a pre-assessment and on-going assessment, you can use the resulting data to develop an instructional roadmap. That map prepares you to understand and build on students' prior knowledge as you plan instruction. It also enables you to be aware of and directly target any misconceptions students may hold. Simply said, to help a student continue to grow in any content sequence, you need to know where the student is at a given time in a learning progression.

Returning to the earlier golf example, a pre-assessment might reveal that while Carlos has never played golf before, he has had experiences with baseball, and his familiarity with batting prepared him for shifting the plane of his swing in golf. Tomas, we might learn, has had no prior experience in either sport and so the biomechanics of swinging at balls is completely new to him. Had the teacher merely surveyed the students about their general familiarity with golf before the unit began, neither boy would have indicated that they had prior knowledge or experience. Rather, having a more nuanced approach to identifying prior knowledge might provide a more insightful picture.

One way to obtain more precise insights is to differentiate the pre-assessment—providing multiple ways to show readiness and experiences related to golf ranging from an interview with the teacher about a student's background experiences in sports; asking students to analyze a short video showing a golfer swing a club; or asking students to swing a bat or club to hit a variety of balls. Through each pathway the student would likely provide a different type of information related to the sport and give the teacher a clearer pathway forward for each student.

The following scenario sets the stage for another example of how gathering data to help make better instructional decisions might look:

Ms. Willis knew that in the upcoming weeks, her high school English class would be studying Shakespeare. Based on her previous experience

with teaching Shakespearean literature, she knew her students would likely come to the unit with all kinds of experiences, knowledge, interests, and attitudes about Shakespeare. As class was ending a few days prior to the start of the Shakespeare unit, Ms. Willis asked students to jot down what they knew about Shakespeare and what experiences they had had with his work. She reminded them that if they didn't know anything about Shakespeare, that was okay—and that their responses would help her know how to plan the unit more effectively. When Ms. Willis looked at the students' responses, she saw a great deal of variation. Some responses to the first question were accurate (for example, the time during which he was born, names of plays he had written, and that he acted in many of his plays). A few responses went beyond baseline information (for example, that his themes applied to people in all times and places, that he had a deep understanding of human nature and human emotions, and that his plays were adapted for various cultures, times, and media). Other responses were inaccurate (e.g., he wrote novels, he lived about 100 years ago), revealed student apprehension (his plays were too hard to understand or didn't connect with modern people). As Ms. Willis read their responses to the second question, she saw that some students had seen live performances of Shakespeare—some even at the Globe Theater, that some knew West Side Story was an adaptation of Romeo and Juliet, and that a few students knew about Shakespearian adaptations in countries from which they had emigrated to the U.S. Some students turned in blank pages. Using the students' responses from this pre-assessment and her growing knowledge about them as individuals, Ms. Willis began to envision ways she might plan the unit to connect with students' varied experiences, entry points, cultures, interests, and concerns so each student could grow in understanding and appreciation of Shakespeare's enduring legacy.

Part of Ms. Willis' considerations for her instruction after reviewing her students' exit tickets is to decide how she will support students during instruction so that each has the full opportunity to master the upcoming unit's learning goals. Ms. Willis should note her students' variation related to prior knowledge with Shakespeare with the range of insights about his work from none to shallow to emerging insights. From this conclusion, she proactively plans for ways to provide instructional experiences—recognizing these will be different for different students. Understanding the concept of ZPD (1978) developed by the Soviet psychologist, Lev Vygotsky, is helpful in planning how to address both the cognitive and affective variation that Ms. Willis finds in the exit tickets.

Zone of Proximal Development as Central to Learning Growth

Vygotsky's (1978) ZPD has, in large measure, shaped our current understanding that a student learns by building on his or her own prior knowledge. Vygotsky's defined ZPD as "the distance between the actual development level as determined by independent problem solving and the level of potential development as determined through problem solving under adult guidance or in collaboration with more capable peer" (p. 86). The ZPD can be characterized from both a cognitive and affective perspective. From the cognitive perspective you want to ensure that the content that students engage with is neither too difficult nor easy. From the affective perspective, having content too difficult or easy results in boredom or being confused and frustrated, which lead to student distraction or lack of motivation to engage. Importantly to note as well is that the optimal conditions for learning differ for each student and can differ for the same students in different contexts. Figure 2.1 displays visually the relationship between the concept of ZPD and differentiation.

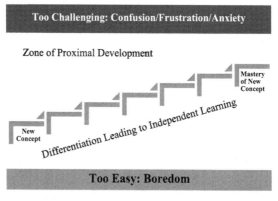

Figure 2.1 The relationship between differentiation and ZPD

Increasing Task Difficulty

Vygotsky (1978) theorized that a learner grows in knowledge, understanding, and skills by working with tasks at his or her current level of development (ZPD), as well as with scaffolding and support necessary to progress to a next level of learning. Similarly, Roosevelt (2008) proposed that students work in their ZPD with learning activities that are interesting and culturally meaningful to them, that are slightly more difficult than they can accomplish alone, and with peer/adult collaboration or scaffolding would enable them to close the gap between the manageable and the slightly out-of-reach. The premise is that after a student successfully completes a learning activity with a competent peer or adult support, or other appropriate scaffolding, he or she is then able to complete the task individually in the next encounter. By continuing this process, the student is able to learn progressively more difficult material. More recently, neuroscientists have shared the physiology behind the psychologists' observations. People learn, neuroscientists say, when the work we ask them to do is moderately challenging. When work is too demanding, the brain is over-taxed and unable to process the new information or skill. When work is too easy, no learning occurs because there is nothing new for the brain to make sense of (Sousa & Tomlinson, 2018; Willis, 2010). The concept of moderate challenge is individual-specific, not class-specific.

Using an example familiar to many, Judy Willis (2010), both a neuroscientist and an educator, explains how teaching students just beyond their current levels of challenge in a continually escalating cycle benefits learning:

> The compelling nature of computer games is an excellent example of differentiating instruction to the students' ZPD...The most popular computer games take players through increasingly challenging levels. As skill improves, the next challenge motivates practice and persistence because the player feels challenge is achievable. Similar incremental, achievable challenges in the classroom, at the appropriate level for students' (current) abilities, are motivating and build mastery by lowering the barrier, not the bar.

(pp. 44–46)

The ideas of ZPD and moderate challenge should inform classroom assessment in the same. In other words, an assessment, just as a lesson, should ask a student to stretch just a bit—and should support the student in doing so. Assessments that are completely out of reach for a student are highly likely to be unproductive and negative for that student. It is unlikely that they will act as catalysts for further growth. Similarly, assessments that only asks student to repeat what has long been familiar to the student are a waste of that student's time—a lost learning opportunity. Thus, pre-assessments and on-going assessments that make room for the entry points of a range of learners will be more effective in helping a teacher target students' ZPDs for instructional planning than pre-assessments and formative assessments that do not make room for student variance. One mechanism that can help teachers plan effectively to address a range of student readiness through pre-assessment, formative assessment, and instruction is the use learning progressions.

Learning Progressions as Tools for Differentiating Assessments and Instruction

Learning progressions are pathways that students might take to reach the end goal contained in the content standards or other learning targets. A learning progression is "a carefully sequenced set of building blocks that students must master en route to mastering a more distant curricular aim" (Popham, 2007). In other words, learning progressions provide the building blocks to standards. That is, they outline the movement toward understanding, although the movement in most instances is not a lock-step sequence of steps (Hess, 2008). Instruction is the process by which students move along the pathway and assessment allows the teacher to know where students are at a specific point in time, a sociocognitive approach to teaching and assessing students' understandings as they develop proficiency with the content (Penuel & Shepard, 2016). What is important is that you use content learning progressions that map onto the curricular program of study. In most cases, this defaults to the state standards as a proxy for the curriculum, but as we noted in Chapter 1, standards are not synonymous with curriculum.

Learning progressions are also helpful when mapping learning targets in other programs such as Advanced Placement (AP) and International Baccalaureate (IB) courses, as well as more "open" curriculum such as Montessori. A mathematics learning progression developed around the Common Core is not the same as a learning standard developed around the Virginia Standards of Learning or the Texas Essential Knowledge and Skills Standards (TEKS). Common to all learning progressions is that they span across ages or grade levels and clearly articulate what students should know and be able to do at specified points in their K-12 educational experiences. The progressions are organized by content areas (e.g., mathematics, science) and provide a roadmap for more complex, challenging, and sophisticated content. These detailed progressions provide guideposts for teachers to address a wider range of academic readiness around a given topic.

Learning progressions answer questions such as "In what order should I teach these skills?" "Which skills develop earlier and which later during a given grade or age group?" "Where might I focus students when they are lagging behind at a particular point—or when they are ahead of most of their peers?" An example of the relevancy of learning progressions for instructional and assessment planning is demonstrated by the following primary mathematics scenario:

In Mr. Hawkins' primary classroom, one of the units that his students will be learning is about money. Mr. Hawkins knows that coming to understand money can be a difficult concept for students because while decimals are involved, money is not a true decimal. Rather money is based on a face value system (i.e., the value of coins and dollars). In order to help him plan for both instruction and assessment appropriate for the unit, Mr. Hawkins identifies a learning progression in primary numeracy involving money[1]:

LP#1: Students are able to match similar coins or dollars in a pile of coins or dollars.

LP#2: Students are able to recognize different coins based on their face value (e.g., 1 cent (penny), 5 cents (nickel), 10 cents (dime), etc.).

LP3#: Students are able to sort and count the number of coins with the same face value.

LP#4: Students are able to count the value of 10 coins of the same value.

LP#5: Students are able to count the value of $5 using coins of the same value.

LP#6: Students are able to the value of $5 using different combination of coins with different values.

LP#7: Students are able to correctly give change using complementary addition between two amounts.

In the case of Mr. Hawkins' money unit, he can adjust students' starting places in the unit based upon pre-assessment data and in accordance with the learning progression sequence.

In designing pre-assessments and on-going assessments that enable a range of learners to show what they currently know, understand, and can do, it is quite helpful for teachers to design questions or prompts that reflect a progression from past to future expectations for student learning. Doing so gives most, if not all, students a chance to reflect on what they comfortably know and to stretch a bit to illustrate their current upper limits of knowledge. In other words, if the assessment samples knowledge along a continuum of development, results from the assessment are likely to help the teacher place students on that continuum more accurately. In turn, the teacher can create instructional sequences designed to meet students at their varied entry points as the unit begins.

The Social Environment as a Catalyst for Learning

A century or more of research in the cognitive sciences confirms that students learn best and make more significant learning gains in a social classroom environment (e.g., Chaiklin, 2003; John-Steiner & Mahn, 1996; National Research Council, 2000). This suggests that students fare best when there is a variety of interactions that allow learners to engage in active learning that leads to understanding. These interactions include meaningful teacher-to-student, student-to-student, small groups, and whole class interactions taking place consistently, over time.

Revisiting the Shakespeare scenario, Ms. Willis uses a variety of grouping configurations to engage her students. These configurations range from whole class discussions to small group work that includes such strategies as a Tea Party, Turn and Talks, Think-Pair-Square-Share, learning stations designed around data she collected through the pre-assessment, concept mapping, peer review, and jigsaw groups. Designed effectively, these strategies create social moments when students engage in conversation and explore varied perspectives on the content they are learning as they navigate toward mastery of designated learning goals.

Additionally, research suggests that the more socially relevant a classroom environment is, the more motivated students are to engage with activities, thus increasing the probability of their learning (e.g., Ryan & Patrick, 2001). Socially relevance within an environment is evident in several distinct, dimensions: student belief that the teacher cares and supports them, interaction among classmates, a general atmosphere created by the teacher that promotes mutual respect and social harmony, and de-emphasis on competition among students—that is, de-emphasis on a performance focus (e.g., Butler, 1995). This sociocultural perspective of student learning is viewed as an interaction between the student and the social environment where the student both shapes and is shaped by the environment (i.e., community of practice; James, 2006). Because students learn through interactions with others while engaged in relevant instructional activities, the focus of assessment becomes about gathering data in order to adapt instruction to improve future learning rather than measuring past performance (Penuel & Shepard, 2016).

Feedback and the Socially Relevant Classroom

In the socially relevant classroom environment, emphasis has been placed on creating instructional opportunities that actively engage students with both the teacher and their peers. However, the socially relevant classroom environment also includes active engagement of both teacher and students in the feedback process. Teachers provide feedback for students, and discuss the feedback with students as needed, to guide their particular next steps in learning. Students review and plan the action they will take based on the written and conversational feedback. Students also review one another's work based on clear guidelines and criteria, incorporating that feedback as appropriate in their own learning plans. (For more information on using peer feedback for learning, see Topping, 2018.) Teachers guide, observe, and coach the peer feedback process, leading the teacher to expand his or her understanding of how students think about, understand, and act on feedback. Research on feedback has also identified several key ways in which feedback can (and should) serve as a tool to further student learning (e.g., Hattie, 2009; Hattie & Timperley, 2007):

1. Feedback allows students the opportunity to understand the intent of identified learning goals which gives students a greater opportunity to reach the goals.
2. Descriptive feedback provides quality information to students about their current learning and identifies what the student needs to do to continue to move along the targeted learning trajectory.
3. Peer feedback enables students to develop metacognitive thinking, which has a positive impact on the student's own work as well as on the work of peers with whom that student interacts.
4. Feedback provides opportunities to close the gap between current and desired performance.
5. Feedback provides information to teachers to shape instruction for students of differing readiness levels as opposed to planning one-size-fits-all instruction.

Looking Back and Ahead

Teaching is both an art and a science. The more fully teachers understand the principles of both those facets, the more positively they can impact student learning in their present as well as future lives. This chapter has explored five conclusions from education science that help us teach more students more effectively—and that help more students learn more fully. Understanding the importance of growth mindset, building new knowledge on past knowledge, ZPD and moderate challenge, learning progressions, and social classroom environments provides teachers with clear guidance for creating classrooms that respond effectively to students' diverse learning needs through differentiating both instruction and assessment to capitalize on students' current knowledge and to move them ahead in a trajectory of learning efficiently and effectively and with enhanced motivation to learn.

Note

1 Based on a Numeracy Progression from the Australian Curriculum, Assessment, and Reporting Authority (ACARA).

References

Aronson, J., Fried, C. B., & Good, C. (2002). Reducing the effects of stereotype threat on African American college students by shaping theories of intelligence. *Journal of Experimental Social Psychology, 38*, 113–125. doi: 10.1006/jesp.2001.1491.

Blackwell, L. S., Trzensniewski, K. H., & Dweck, C. S. (2007). Implicit theories of intelligence predict achievement across an adolescent transition: A longitudinal study and an intervention. *Child Development, 78*, 246–263.

Butler, R. (1995). Motivational informational functions and consequences of children's attention to peers' work. *Journal of Educational Psychology, 87*, 347–360.

Chaiklin, S. (2003). The zone of proximal development in Vygotsky's theory of learning and school instruction. In A. Kozulin, B. Gindis, V. S. Ageyev, & S. M. Miller (Eds.), *Vygotsky's educational theory in cultural context* (pp. 39–64). Cambridge, UK: Cambridge University Press.

Claro, S., Paunesku, D., & Dweck, C. S. (2016). Growth mindset tempers the effects of poverty on academic achievement. *Proceedings of the National Academy of Sciences, 113*, 8664–8668. doi: 10.1073/pnas.1608207113.

Darling-Hammond, L., Flook, L., Cook-Harvey, C., Barron, B., & Osher, D. (2019). Implications for educational practice of the science of learning and development. *Applied Developmental Science.* doi: 10.1080/10888691.2018.1537791.

Degol, J. L., Wang, M. T., Zhang, Y., & Allerton, J. (2018). Do growth mindsets in math benefit females? Identifying pathways between gender, mindset, and motivation. *Journal of Youth and Adolescence, 47*, 976–990. doi:10.1007/s10964-017-0739-8.

Dweck, C. S. (2006). *Mindset: The new psychology of success.* New York, NY: Random House.

Hattie, J. (2009). *Visible learning: A synthesis of over 800 meta-analyses relating to achievement.* New York, NY: Routledge.

Hattie, J., & Timperley, H. (2007). The power of feedback. *Review of Educational Research, 77*, 81–112. doi:10.3102%2F003465430298487.

Hess, K. (2008). *Developing and using learning progressions as a schema for measuring progress.* Dover, NH: National Center for Assessment. Retrieved from https://www.nciea.org/publications/CCSSO2_KH08.pdf.

James, M. (2006). Assessment, teaching, and theories of learning. In J. Gardner (Ed.), *Assessment and learning* (pp. 47–60). London, UK: Sage Publications.

John-Steiner, V., & Mahn, H. (1996). Sociocultural approaches to learning and development: A Vygotskian framework. *Educational Psychologist, 31*, 191–206.

Lenroot, R. K., & Giedd, J. N. (2007). The structural development of the human brain as measured longitudinally with magnetic resonance imaging. In D. Coch, K. W. Fischer, & Dawson, G. (Eds.), *Human behavior, learning, and the developing brain. Typical development* (pp. 50–73). New York, NY: Guilford Press.

McMillan, J. H. (2016). Section discussion: Student perceptions of assessment. In G. T. L. Brown & L. R. Harris (Eds.), *Handbook of human and social conditions in assessment* (pp. 221–243). New York, NY: Routledge.

National Research Council. (2000). *How people learn: Brain, mind, experience, and school: Expanded edition.* Washington, DC: The National Academies Press. doi: 10.17226/9853.

Ng, B. (2018). The neuroscience of growth mindset and intrinsic motivation. *Brain Sciences, 8*(2). doi: 10.3390/brainsci8020020. Retrieved from https://www.ncbi.nlm.nih.gov/pmc/articles/PMC5836039/.

Penuel, W. R., & Shepard, L. A. (2016). Assessment and teaching. In D. H. Gitomer & C. A. Bell (Eds.), *Handbook of research on teaching* (pp. 787–850). Washington, DC: AERA.

Popham, W. J. (2007). All about accountability / The lowdown on learning progressions. *Educational Leadership, 64*, 83–84.

Rattan, A., Good, C., & Dweck, C. S. (2012). "It's ok – not everyone can be good at math": Instructors with an entity theory comfort (and demotivate) students. *Journal of Experimental Social Psychology, 48*, 731–737. doi: 10.1016/j.jesp.2011.12.012.

Roosevelt, F. D. (2008). Zone of proximal development. In N. J. Salkind (Ed.), *Encyclopedia of Educational Psychology* (pp. 1017–1022). Thousand, Oaks, CA: SAGE. doi: 10.4135/9781412963848.0282. Retrieved from https://sk.sagepub.com/reference/educational psychology/n282.xml.

Ryan, A., & Patrick, H. (2001). The classroom social environment and changes in adolescents' motivation and engagement during middle school. *American Educational Research Journal, 38*, 437–460. doi: 10.3102%2F00028312038002437.

Schunk, D. H. (2016). *Learning theories: An educational perspective* (7th Ed.). London, UK: Pearson.

Siegle, D., McCoach, D. B., & Roberts, A. (2017). Why I believe I achieve determines whether I achieve. *High Ability Studies, 28*, 59–72. doi: 10.1080/13598139.2017.1302873.

Smith, T., Brumskill, R., Johnson, A., & Zimmer, T. (2018). The impact of teacher language on students' mindsets and statistics performance. *Social Psychology of Education, 21*, 775–786. doi: 10.1007/s11218-018-9444-z.

Sousa, D., & Tomlinson, C. (2018). *Differentiation and the brain: How neuroscience supports the learner-friendly classroom* (2nd Ed.). Bloomington, IN: Solution Tree.

Topping, K. (2018). *Using peer assessment to inspire reflection and learning.* New York, NY: Routledge.

Vygotsky, L. S. (1978). *Mind in society: The development of higher psychological processes.* Cambridge, MA: Harvard University Press.

Walton, G. M., & Cohen, G. L. (2011). A brief social-belonging intervention improves academic and health outcomes of minority students. *Science, 6023*, 1447–1451. doi: 10.1126/science.1198364.

Willis, J. (2010). The current impact of neuroscience on teaching and learning. In D. Sousa (Ed.), *Mind brain, and education* (47–67). Bloomington, IN: Solution Tree.

Yeager, D. S., & Dweck, C. S. (2012). Mindsets that promote resilience: When students believe that personal characteristics can be developed. *Educational Psychologist, 47*, 302–314. doi: 10.1080/00461520.2012.722805.

ZelaZo, P. D., Blair, C. B., & Willoughby, M. T. (2017). *Executive function: Implications for education* (NCER 2017-2000). Washington, DC: National Center for Education Research, Institute of Education Sciences, U.S. Department of Education. Retrieved from http://ies.ed.gov.

3

Differentiated Formative Assessment

In this chapter, we share principles that guide preparation for creating useful formative assessments, and offer a series of guiding questions to inform the examination and interpretation of formative assessment results to enhance differentiation. We look at examples of formative assessment that occur at the beginning of the cycle (pre-assessment) as well as the formative assessment that occurs in tandem with instruction (on-going assessment). After each we suggest ways in which you can apply what is learned from differentiated formative assessments to inform student groupings, adjust instructional plans, and serve as a mirror for both student and teacher reflection. In addition, we will consider ways in which you can differentiate the formative assessments themselves to optimize what is learned about the students in order to generate instructional plans that are likely to be effective for a broad range of learners.

Linking Curriculum, Assessment, and Instruction

The assessment cycle is a process within a broader instructional cycle, and it serves as the linchpin between curriculum and instruction. The earliest stage of preparing for meaningful assessment takes place well before most teachers are thinking about the assessments themselves. Fundamental to student learning success is a teacher thoughtfully identifying the knowledge, understanding, and skills that will be the focal points of teaching and learning. This step is foundational for establishing what should become a "three-part harmony" among curriculum, assessment, and instruction.

To create that harmony, teachers begin by identifying the standards and the specific curricular content through which they will teach those standards to determine the essential knowledge (information), understandings (big ideas or principles), and skills for a learning sequence. It is important to recall that the list of standards is not a curriculum. Likewise, a textbook is not a curriculum. Rather, a curriculum is the detailed roadmap to help students explore, engage with, make sense of, and be able to use important knowledge and skills around a particular focus area. This detailed map outlines four basic components: (1) the content learning goals, including the big ideas and essential questions, guiding the unit of study; (2) the specific instructional methods broken down into individual lessons composed of relevant content that are driven by learning objectives and that are ordered in a meaningful way to build toward the unit's big ideas; (3) the materials (e.g., textbook, media, trade books, websites) that are used by the teacher and students to facilitate the teaching, learning, and transfer of the content; and (4) an assessment plan that includes both formative and summative assessments.

While a list of standards and a textbook may be necessary ingredients for a curriculum, they are not the complete academic plan by any means. Even when standards or other learning goals are provided for teachers, they do not delineate knowledge (Ks), understandings (Us), and skills (Ds). Many, if not most standards are presented as skills and very few provide understandings. For this reason, a key step in curricular planning for teachers is to analyze the standards and other documents to determine the necessary Ks), Us and Ds adding or adapting KUDs based on their own content knowledge and knowledge of the students they are likely to teach. Another powerful element in the art of teaching is knowing how to craft learning sequences and experiences that will be relevant and engaging for students while simultaneously calling on them to master the learning goals. In short, the first principle in creating meaningful formative assessments is careful determination and delineation of essential KUDs.

Alignment of Targeted KUDs with Appropriate Formative Assessment Strategies

Once KUDs are established, the teacher plans formative assessments that align tightly with the KUDs so that these measures provide useful windows into student learning and growth over time. Formative assessments have been categorized into three types, all of which contribute to the learning cycle (Heritage, 2007; Tomlinson & Moon, 2013): (1) "on the fly," which are informal assessments that happen during a lesson and allow for a teacher to get a "group reading" on how things are going at a particular moment; (2) "planned for interaction" where an assessment is pre-planned to gather informative data (e.g., pre-assessment; end-of-lesson exit tickets; journaling); and (3) "curriculum embedded" which are summative assessments used to specifically gather data at significant points in a curriculum unit during the learning process (e.g., a quiz after lesson 4). Aligning the assessment process with the KUDs requires identifying the specific assessment process for gathering the data and how that strategy aligns with the targeted KUDs. Table 3.1 offers examples of this alignment between learning objectives and assessment strategy.

For example, if the learning objective is simply about recall or recognition, then the most appropriate assessment strategy is an objective type of assessment where students fill in the blanks, respond to multiple choice questions, label diagrams, or recite orally or in writing. In contrast, if the intent is to gather evidence of student understanding, different types of assessment

Table 3.1 Alignment between Learning Objective and Assessment Strategy

Type of Learning Objective—KUD	Appropriate Assessment Strategy
Knowledge (e.g., Identify, Recall, Recognize)	Objective items such as fill-in-the-blanks, multiple choice, matching, or labeling
Understanding	Problem where students create concept maps, summarize, compare and contrast, classify or categorize, paraphrase
Skills (Apply, Implement, Execute)	Problems that require students to use procedures to solve task (e.g., simulations, labs, performances)

strategies are used. Assessment scenarios that ask students to create a concept map, or compare and contrast two events, policies, or points of view, or summarize readings, analyze speeches are all ways that allow student understanding to be observed and measured. If you intend to measure students' application of knowledge, understandings, and skills, then the assessment should invite students to demonstrate those elements either singly or in combination with other skills, such as demonstrating, performing, or simulating what a problem solving task would look like in authentic settings.

While it is not always the case that formative assessments are differentiated, it is likely that the teacher will have clearer, and therefore more useful, information about the status of the class as a whole and of individual students relative to the KUDs if the assessments are differentiated. Therefore, planning assessments may, at least on occasion, involve differentiating some aspects of the assessments.

Administering and Interpreting Formative Assessment Data

The last step in preparing the assessment is administering it. Regardless of the form it takes, the teacher asks students to share what they know, understand, and can do at a point in time within the unit. Students should understand that the more fully they are able to demonstrate their developing knowledge, the more helpful the assessment will be to the teacher in planning effectively for their continued growth—and the more useful it will be to them in knowing how to plan for their own success. This can occur as you talk with students about the purpose of formative assessment, as you demonstrate to students how the assessments are used to improve teaching and learning. In other words, you need to show to students that the formative assessment process contributes to higher achievement and success on summative assessments.

Once students have completed the assessment, your next step is to review the students' work, looking for patterns in the data. This does not have to be an extensive process. When the assessment is clearly focused on a subset of KUDs, student responses should signal their strengths, gaps, and misconceptions with those KUDs. After a few rounds of reviewing formative "snapshots" of student progress based on KUDs, teachers are likely to find the process of looking for and finding patterns in the data to be fairly straightforward. Making sense of the patterns in the data is a necessary step before using the information to guide decision-making. Finally, you can use the data from an assessment to reveal where each student is in his or her development with the KUDs as the unit moves along in order to plan instruction that is both consistently well-aligned with the KUDs and aligned with the various needs of learners in the class.

Guiding Questions

To facilitate linking the components in the curriculum, assessment, instruction cycle, it is helpful to address a series of guiding questions. Starting with the clearly articulated learning goals (KUDs), first ask, where are we in the learning cycle? Are we just getting started in a new unit of study or is this a series of learning experiences that have been occurring over time? In short, ask, "What's my purpose in assessing students?" Next, consider, "What do I need to know? What am I trying to figure out?" Once armed with data it is essential to identify patterns and find meaning in what you learn. A teacher makes sense of the available data by asking, *"What does the data mean?"* The most essential step in this process is to translate the lessons learned into actionable steps to inform instruction. In other words, ask yourself, *"Now that I see patterns, what do I do?"* These guiding questions inform the process of gathering useful data to guide instructional decisions, such as: *"I need to re-teach these Ks, Us, and Ds to these students," "I now recognize that these students are ready for additional challenges,"* and *"I'm now going to find opportunities to connect these ideas and skills to the students interests I just discovered."*

Now that we have explored the cycle in generalities, let's look closer at the first stage in the curriculum-assessment-instruction cycle—the pre-assessment. In the following section, we examine what happens at the beginning of the assessment process and consider a specific teacher's approach using the guiding questions.

Pre-Assessing to Guide Future Instruction

As noted in Chapter 1, the first phase of the assessment cycle is known as pre-assessment, a special category of formative assessment that is designed to give teachers data to inform decisions prior to starting a new instructional unit. It is unique from other formative assessments because this type of assessment precedes the beginning of a new unit or topic of study. Pre-assessment data are most helpful when they are focused at the individual student level because they give you insights about each student. These insights in turn allow you to determine if what was about to be covered in the upcoming unit is already mastered, and if so, by whom. The insights also can identify gaps that students may have and that may in turn impede their learning of the new content (i.e., pre-requisite knowledge, understandings, and/or skills). Both of these instances signal to you to need for differentiation. Finally, pre-assessments give students a preview of what is about to be covered, thus making clear to them what they should be striving to learn. Knowing this information about the upcoming new content in turn allows students to be more active participants in the learning process.

There are numerous forms that the pre-assessment can take, from formal paper-and-pencil pre-tests, to informal entrance/exit tickets, focused journal prompts, or, with very young students, language learners, or students with other particular challenges, one-on-one questions or hands-on tasks that can reach these students' knowledge, understanding, and skill. Administration of the pre-assessment need not be time-consuming. You can administer the pre-assessment at a single point in time, or collect the information over time by adding items to other assignments or collecting exit tickets across several days. Regardless of how it takes shape, a pre-assessment should be: (1) focused at the individual student level; (2) intentional in targeting specific learning goals, which may include pre-requisite knowledge and skills; and (3) conducted prior to the start of a new unit of study.

While it would be convenient to imagine that data from pre-assessments would shape all decisions for a forthcoming unit, that likely will not be the case. It is important to avoid "over-reaching" conclusions about students' needs for an upcoming unit too early in the learning process. Instead, the goal is to gather just enough information to begin the new unit with some insight about students' readiness to begin, to inform initial grouping configurations, to inform early choices of materials to be used, and/or to adjust entry points into the unit. Here is an example of a teacher using guiding questions, as the unit begins, to inform his planning:

In preparing for an upcoming unit of Weather and Climate, Mr. Rivers knows that many of his former students held misconceptions about weather and climate science at the outset because of similar units he taught them. Table 3.3 provides the KUDs for the unit. He also realizes that many of the student misconceptions come from exposure to several different sources both inside and outside of school: April 2 each year when TV coverage highlights Punxsutawney Phil and whether he sees his shadow (all based on superstition derived from the Pennsylvania Dutch), or family members reading and following predictions from the Old Farmer's Almanac, or from emoji forecasting from smartphones, or even from the explanation that was provided in an earlier grade textbook. Ironically, many educators (and consequentially students) don't realize that weather forecasting and climate science are based heavily in sophisticated analyses surrounding advanced mathematics, physics, thermodynamics, and fluid dynamics. And while Mr. Rivers will not tackle these advanced topics in his 7th grade classroom, he does want to have some evidence of what his students' perceived ideas about weather and climate are and why they think as they do. A few weeks in advance of the unit starting, Mr. Rivers asks students one question as they prepare to exit the classroom: What is the difference between climate and day-to-day weather?

Data Interpretation Process

The process of interpreting pre-assessment data is based on several considerations. First, you need to know if the data align with the purpose for gathering it. In the above example, Mr. Rivers wants to know what misconceptions students may have about weather and climate because he understands that not addressing those misconceptions at the outset of the new unit will hinder students from mastering the learning goals for the unit. Additionally, he anticipates that students will share information that will allow him to determine what pre-requisite scientific information may need to be revisited, as well as areas where students have deeper levels of understanding of scientific content. For these reasons, he chooses a single question for his pre-assessment. As noted earlier, the pre-assessment can be brief and not time consuming to administer.

Second, you need to be able to draw accurate conclusions from the data. Mr. Rivers needs to be able to sort and compare the data from the students' responses to determine which students have no obvious misconceptions about weather and climate, which students revealed misconceptions about the topics, and which students' responses made interpretation about their understandings (or lack thereof) difficult to determine. Being able to draw accurate conclusions from the student data involves first generating overall impressions of students' responses, specifically looking in general terms where students differed. Questions that Mr. Rivers might ask as he looks through the gathered data from exit cards could include: *How well did the class do as a whole (e.g., how many students responded to the question with reasonable accuracy, how many students revealed misconceptions, and how many students revealed that they knew nothing about the two terms)?* The "grand tour" question gives Mr. Rivers a sense of the overall class performance, or a snapshot of the class, as well as a sense of the entry points of individuals and small clusters of students. If the data indicate that the students have prior knowledge that is accurate and is not impacted by misunderstandings, this informs where, within the trajectory of knowledge, Mr. Rivers will begin the unit. For example, if all of his students' responses indicated that they could accurately distinguish between weather and climate, Mr. Rivers would begin the unit in a different way than if a set of students' responses indicated misconceptions and/or inaccurate information. In the latter case, Mr. Rivers would need to provide that set of students with opportunities to explore prior relevant concepts that may have contributed to the inaccurate information. In that case he would then ask: *Who are the specific students demonstrating understanding of the two terms and who are the specific students demonstrating misconceptions? Who are the students whose blank or irrelevant responses invite further investigation?*

Knowing which students did and did not answer the pre-assessment correctly alerts Mr. Rivers to the fact that starting instruction at the same place for the class as a whole will not be a fit for all the students. As a result, he needs to consider the appropriate starting place for the group of students who responded correctly, the instructional starting place for the students who held misconceptions, or did not respond. Being able to answer these questions with data informs the initial groupings of students (no obvious misunderstandings, misunderstandings, more information needed), as well as the differentiated content of the first few lessons. It also might be the case that his first lessons are designed to raise interest, confidence and curiosity in the study of climate science and the differentiated lessons would begin a few lessons later, allowing him to gather even more insights into the students along the way.

The Data Meaning-Making template for Mr. Rivers might look like the one in Table 3.2.

Table 3.2 Data Interpretation Template

LEARNING TARGETS:		
Know:		
Understandings:		
Skills:		
What's the Purpose:		
Here's What I Know about What the Students Know Understand and Can Do	*What Does This Mean about What Students Know, Understand, and Can Do?*	*Now What? Implications for Instruction*
Each supported with specific evidence from the data	What does the evidence tell me about student learning status on the KUDs?	

Answering the "*Now What?*" question requires Mr. Rivers to consider the content that needs to be taught. With the group that held misconceptions, the content should be re-introduced to the students; in the group that responded correctly to the question Mr. Rivers must consider what (new) content should be introduced; and for the group that did not respond to the question, Mr. Rivers plans to connect with the students to see what they know and don't know. Answering these questions requires Mr. Rivers to consider:

- the content/learning targets for each group;
- the instructional strategy to use to allow students access to the content;
- the materials needed for both the teaching of the content and for the students to interact with to make sense of the content; and
- the plan for managing groups so that each group successful achieves the intended learning.

Table 3.3 KUDs for 7th Grade Weather and Climate Unit

Unit: 7th grade Weather & Climate (www.nextgenscience.org)
KUDs:
K: Vocabulary (weather, climate, air masses, air pressure, temperature, humidity)
U: Cause and effect relationships may be used to predict phenomena in natural or designed systems. Air masses flow from regions of high to low pressure causing weather at a fixed location to change over time. Sudden changes in weather can result when different air masses collide. Weather can be predicted within probabilistic ranges
D: Collect and interpret data; Develop and use a model to explain weather conditions

Assessment Purpose: To inform the upcoming unit; identify misconceptions		
Here's What I Know about What the Students Know, Understand, and Can Do	*What Does This Mean about What Students Know, Understand, and Can Do?*	*Now What?*

The example of Mr. Rivers demonstrates how assessment data can be used to inform differentiated instructional responses. In the following section, we'll look closer at the second stage in the curriculum-assessment-instruction cycle—on-going assessment. As with the example above, we examine what how the guiding questions can support a teacher's on-going assessment practices.

Using On-going Assessment Data for Differentiating Instruction

A second form of formative assessment occurs *during* instruction. On-going assessment is defined as data that are collected formally or informally to help guide subsequent instruction *within* a learning cycle (e.g., while teaching the unit occurs).

This on-going collection of data includes a variety of data types, ranging from analyzing student work, engaging in conversations with students about what they are learning, observing students engaging in learning activities as well as conducting more formal assessments, such as quizzes. Unlike pre-assessments, these data may be considered at the individual student level (e.g., analyzing student work) or across a group to gauge the general status of the group with targeted KUDs for "on-the-fly" adjustments. For example, you may ask students to give a "thumbs up" or "thumbs down" or "thumbs sideways" to show how confident they feel with the lesson at that moment.

To Grade or Not to Grade On-going Assessments

In general, on-going assessments are providing feedback for two audiences: (1) to give you as the teacher actionable feedback about where your students stand relative to the targeted learning goals as well as providing information on the success of your instruction; and (2) to give students information about what concepts they performed well on and which ones they did not, the types of mistakes they made so that similar mistakes can be avoided in the future, and to give actionable feedback about how they can better prepare to learn the targeted learning goals or similar learning goals in the future. The question that comes up is whether these types of assessments will be graded. While there is disagreement in the field about whether formative assessments are graded or not, there are points of agreement about grading in general: (1) grading and assessment serve different purposes and are not interchangeable; (2) grading student work is not essential to student learning (Lipnevich & Smith, 2008); (3) there exists no one perfect grading system as each has its unique drawbacks (Brookhart & Nitko, 2019; McMillan, Myran, & Workman, 2002); (4) grading should be done in reference to learning criteria (Muñoz & Guskey, 2015); (5) grading has no value in being used as punishment if learning is the goal; and (6) grading is inherently a professional judgment whereby there is a degree of subjectivity involved (Brookhart et al., 2016; Guskey & Jung, 2016). Given these "truths" as background, do you grade on-going assessments? For us, we take the position that "it depends." The answer depends on what the on-going assessment's purpose is, the type of assessment it is, and where it is given in the learning cycle.

On-going assessments differ from pre-assessments in that you would potentially grade the work (albeit properly weighted) under the condition that the on-going assessment is specifically timed to give an indication of the level of mastery of important knowledge, skills, and/or understandings that are required for subsequent topics in a unit. In other words, a formative assessment might be graded when students have had sufficient time and opportunity to learn the material, and when grading the work would be informative to students regarding upcoming summative assessments. For example, you might decide that within a civics unit on civil rights that it would be important to document that students have a firm understanding of the Black Codes (aka as Black Laws) prior to moving into the Jim Crow era. You create a 15-item quiz to be administered after lesson 3 before moving into the Jim Crow era and ultimately the road to civil rights. In this example, the final summative assessment for the unit is a performance task in which students will write an editorial for a school display on how the three branches of the government contributed to the Civil Rights Movement. Students having a grasp of the Black Codes would be important to building their understanding of the Civil Rights Movement.

In the Civil Rights example, the quiz would be appropriately weighted so that it does not make the same contribution to the overall unit grade, as does the performance assessment. The reason for the weighting is so that the quiz has less influence on the overall unit grade because it is only measuring a limited number of learning targets, all of which are required to complete the end-of-unit performance assessment, which is cumulative over the entire unit. It is also noteworthy that in this given example, it would have not been appropriate to differentiate the content of the quiz but that the process by which students accessed or responded to the quiz could be differentiated. In either case, the weighting of the quiz would not be affected by the differentiation.

Let's now examine a teacher who uses on-going assessment to inform her instructional practice (Table 3.4).

Mrs. Brooks' 4th graders are in the middle of a 4-week unit on fractions. Prior to the beginning of the unit, she pre-assessed key concepts that confirmed that students' developmental understandings of fractions varied considerably. From the outset, she made plans for students to progress in the unit in flexible ways. Some students moved ahead into new topics and she met with the group daily to check in about their progress. Meanwhile other students were exploring the fractions with partners or in small groups. After a few days of instruction, the groups shift again. Every day, Mrs. Brooks assembled the class together for "Math Meetings" to discuss real world applications of fractions and to solve a story problem together. All students were able to contribute what they were learning to the discussion and she made careful notes on each student's contributions to interpret

Table 3.4 Learning Targets for the 4th Grade Unit on Fractions

Unit: 4th grade fractions		
KUDs:		
K: Vocabulary (part-part; part-whole, numerator, denominator, quotient, fraction, ratio)		
U: There is a relationship between the whole, the number of parts, and the portion being considered		
D: Represent fractions using models (area, set, number line), narratives, symbols		
What's the Purpose: to identify misconceptions in visualizations before teaching algorithms; inform groupings; adjust instruction based on data		
Here's What I Know about What the Students Know, Understand, and Can Do	*What Does This Mean about What Students Know, Understand, and Can Do?*	*Now What?*

the signals of students' developing understandings. Mrs. Brooks reviewed the notes she took while observing students as they worked together to talk through their logic of problem solving. After today's lesson she asks all of the students to complete an exit ticket:

What is the fraction of black dots to not black dots?[1]

1/6
1/7
1:6
1:7

Something else (specify):

Please explain narratively (or draw a model to show) why you chose your answer

After school, Mrs. Brooks looks at the students' work so she can see the degree of understanding of the part-part vs. part-whole relationships of fractions. This information will guide what she needs to do for the next several classes.

Using the Data Interpretation Process

As in the earlier pre-assessment example, Mrs. Brooks is clear about the specific knowledge and skills that students are studying and she designs an assessment that elicits responses for her specific purpose. In her case, she is interested in seeing how students make sense of part-part and part-whole relationships in fractions and while the assessment itself is not differentiated, students' responses will likely allow her to differentiate her instruction based on their range of responses.

First, the teacher needs to know if it is the right data for her purpose. Mrs. Brooks anticipates that some students may confuse the part-part relationship (i.e., red M&M (1) + not red M&M (6)) and part-whole (i.e., red M&M (1) + the whole set (7)). She is also interested in reading how students came to the answer they selected and provides options for how they "prove" their answer using words or models. Even though students have been working in differentiated work groups based on the initial pre-assessment, Mrs. Brooks intentionally gave a common formative assessment so that she could see evidence of students' developing understandings, which may shift her groups and inform how she plans subsequent lessons.

Second, the teacher needs to be able to draw accurate conclusions from the data. Like Mr. Rivers, Mrs. Brooks needs to scan the class as a whole as well as individuals within it. She needs to identify patterns of students' responses in an efficient manner so that the bulk of energy is applied to meaning making—not sorting through extensive papers. Using a single question allows her to be able to sort and compare the data from the students' responses to determine how students are making meaning of these key concepts of part-part and part-whole. Mrs. Brooks will ask herself questions such as: *How well did the class do as a whole? (e.g., how many students accurately answered the question and offered an accurate explanation in words or pictures? How many students chose the correct answer but offered an incomplete or inaccurate reason? How many students selected the incorrect answer and offered no explanation or offered an explanation that revealed misunderstandings? Which students in the class were in each of these categories? What other unexpected insights emerged from students' explanations? What other errors were committed and if so, by which students?* The answers to these questions will establish potentially new groups of students and will inform how Mrs. Brooks teaches (and demonstrates) content for the next sequence of lessons on fractions. Step 3 outlines examples of appropriate actions that Mrs. Brooks might take in response to student answers.

Unlike with the initial pre-assessment data, this "quick check," administered during instruction, provides insights for Mrs. Brooks a more sophisticated understanding (especially when considered in conjunction with her other formative data from classroom observations and other student-generated work). From here, Mrs. Brooks is well-prepared to adjust not only grouping of students, but instructional materials, pace of instruction, and types of mathematical discourse. From these data she identifies students who have specific misunderstandings or who should be part of a mini-lesson. She also sees ways to modify homework assignments and generates ideas for upcoming Math Meetings.

The Data Meaning-Making template for Mrs. Brooks might look like Table 3.5.

Table 3.5 Data Interpretation Template for Mrs. Brooks 4th Grade Mathematics Class

What's the Purpose: On-going Assessment		
Here's What I Know *Specific Evidence*	What Does This Mean? *Interpretation of the Evidence*	Now What? *Implications for Instruction*
Correct answer and explanation/model	Students who provided a correct answer and explanation suggest they have an understanding of proportional relationships (i.e., relationship between two distinct subgroups).	What are the instructional actions that need to happen for groups:
Answer correct, incorrect explanation/model		• Ready to Move Forward: More formal operations with fractions, using drawings, visual models, and equations to solve problems with fractions.
Incorrect answer and explanation/model	For students who had the correct answer (perhaps because of guessing) but an incorrect explanation *and* for students who had both an incorrect answer more information is needed as to their exact standing within the part-part relationship. Could it be that they don't have a solid understanding of the part-whole relationship?	• Ready for additional Part-Part Relationship OR Re-visit Part-Whole Relationship for "answer only" group, gather more information
No response		
		What resources are needed for each group?
	"No response" students: more information is needed.	What are the management techniques that I will use to ensure that students are working effectively within and across groupings?

Mrs. Brooks' third step is to consider how the responses will shape what happens next—the answer to the "*Now What?*" question. With the group that provided a correct answer but incorrect explanation, the content should be re-introduced to the students; in the group that responded correctly to the question (i.e., both the answer and the explanation), Mrs. Brooks must consider what (new) content should be introduced, and for the two groups that did not respond to the question or provided both an incorrect answer and explanation, Mrs. Brook plans to connect with the students to see what they know and don't know. Specific factors that Mrs. Brooks must consider include:

Content/Learning Targets for Each Group

Mrs. Brooks decides that she will have two groups to start off: the group that provided both the correct answer and explanation, the groups where the explanations were incorrect or no information was provided. Mrs. Brooks decides that the student group that provided a correct answer and explanation is ready to move into more complex manipulations of part-part and part-whole relationships. Her instructional plan will be to continue to build upon students' relational and proportional understanding within the context of performing more formal operations (i.e., addition, subtraction, multiplication) with fractions and mixed numbers, particularly within the context of word problems. She will also continue to engage students in the use of drawings, visual models, and equations.

For the two groups that had incorrect explanations, Mrs. Brooks will first need to consider where the students are relative to their understanding of the part-whole relationship. For students that provide evidence of the part-whole relationship, Mrs. Brooks will return to building students' understanding of the part-part relationship, clearly focusing on what the denominator and numerator indicate within the fractional unit. For others she will focus on re-teaching the topic of partitioning the whole into non-overlapping areas through the use of area, set, and number line models, using approaches that differ in some way from previous approaches which were not successful in helping students solidify their understandings.

Instructional Strategies to Use to Allow Students Access to the Content

Mrs. Brooks will use small groups, where one group will work independently while she works with the other group.

Plans for Managing Groups so that Each Group Successfully Achieves the Intended Learning

Mrs. Brooks will set up a "parking lot" for questions that a student may have while she is working with the other group in order for her not to be disturbed during her micro-teaching moments. She will also have at least three computer stations with video lessons which students can independently access. These video lessons will provide more visual demonstration of the fractional relationships followed by "check-up" questions that will allow Mrs. Brooks to quickly monitor can how well students' are progressing.

Summary

It is important to note that formative assessments may or may not be differentiated. The types of questions that formative assessments pose should provide for a sufficient range of student responses so that instruction, when appropriate, can be differentiated. Having high-quality data from formative assessments for using to guide instruction requires identification what you want to know about your students (i.e., clarity of the targeted learning goals), the opportunities created to administer and collect the data (prior to the unit starting (pre-assessment)) informally during the unit (e.g., on-the-fly) or formally during the unit (e.g., curriculum-embedded); reflection of the evidence that is collected from the administration of the formative assessment (e.g., identifying gaps in students' learning or which students are well above or beyond expectations), and, after reflection, formulation of next instructional steps. Formative assessment serves as the compass for planning effective differentiated instruction.

Note

1 Based on examples retrieved from: https://tapintoteenminds.com/progression-of-fractions/

References

Brookhart, S. M., Guskey, T. R., Bowers, A. J., McMillan, J. H., Smith, J. K., Smith, L. F., ..., & Welsh, M. E. (2016). A century of grading research: Meaning and value in the most common educational measure. *Review of Educational Research, 86*(4), 803–848. doi: 10.3102/0034654316672069

Brookhart, S. M., & Nitko, A. J. (2019). *Educational assessment of students* (8th Ed.). New York: NY: Pearson Publishing.

Guskey, T. R., & Jung, L. A. (2016). Grading: Why you should trust your judgment. *Educational Leadership, 73*(7), 50–54.

Heritage, M. (2007). Formative assessment: What do teachers need to know and do? *Phi Delta Kappan, 89*(2), 140–145. doi: 10.1177/003172170708900210.

Lipnevich, A. A., & Smith, J. K. (2008). *Response to assessment feedback: The effects of grades, praise, and source of information* (ETS RR-08-30). Princeton, NJ: ETS. Retrieved from http://www.ets.org/Media/Research/pdf/RR-08-03.pdf.

McMillan, J. H., Myran, S., & Workman, D. (2002). Elementary teachers' classroom assessment and grading practices. *The Journal of Educational Research, 95*(4), 203–213. doi: 10.1080/00220670209596593.

Muñoz, M. A., & Guskey, T. R. (2015). Standards-based grading and reporting will improve education. *Phi Delta Kappan, 96*(7), 64–68.

Tomlinson, C. A., & Moon, T. R. (2013). *Assessment and student success in a differentiated classroom.* Alexandria, VA: ASCD.

4

Planning for and Using Data from Differentiated Performance Assessments

The third stage in the assessment cycle, known as assessment *of* learning, or summative assessment, involves the consideration and processing of assessment data at the end of a unit of study or at the end of a chunk or subset of a unit of study for the purposes of "summarizing" students' learning up to that point in time. Summative assessments are nearly typically graded because they are given after students have had time to practice the new content and make sense of it. In this chapter, we build upon the guiding principles outlined in Chapter 3 to consider differentiation of the preparation, implementation and interpretation of one type of summative assessment, performance assessment. Often we imagine the traditional pencil and paper "final exam" as the default summative assessment, and in some cases that assessment method is the best fit. In this chapter we delineate how to employ differentiated performance assessment that aligns with the philosophy of differentiation. When well designed and associated to the learning targets, differentiated performance assessment can elicit evidence of student knowledge, understandings, and skills (KUDs) that comprise a unit of study. Performance assessments are also the best way to assess student understanding and facility with applying and/or transferring what they have learned. We conclude this chapter with considerations for grading in order to ensure that the grades are representative of the best thinking surrounding the measurement of student performance.

What Are Summative Assessments?

Summative assessments are assessments *of* learning. They are given periodically to "sum up" or gauge at a particular point in time student learning relative to specific content learning objectives. Taking a pause in instruction to take a snapshot of students' developing knowledge, understanding and skills may occur after a series of lessons on a common topic or at the end of a learning cycle. For example, after completing five lessons associated with one topic of a larger unit, a teacher may administer a formal quiz. The responses on the quiz capture the students' standing at that point in time, and in so doing are "summative" for that first topic of the unit. This type of quiz, which tests a short learning segment, is sometimes called a "Little s" summative assessment. Importantly, this type of assessment also serves a formative function to "course correct" before a "Big S" summative assessment after completing topics 2 and 3 of the unit, or before the final unit test at the end of a reporting period. Examples of "Big S" summative assessments include, but are not limited to, performances, simulations, end-of-unit exams, chapter tests, portfolios, oral exams, culminating projects, and research reports. Because "Big S" assessments happen late in the instructional cycle, the most effective use of data from these assessments is evaluative, rather than to inform instruction.

In addition to providing summative feedback and grades to students, summative assessments can also provide beneficial insights to teachers by helping them see which parts of the unit could benefit from curriculum revisions, improving the teaching and learning for the next instructional cycle. School leaders often find "Big S" assessments useful for illuminating patterns of performance across sub-groups of students within a grade, as well as to compare performance trends across grade levels. Under the right conditions, the data gathered from summative assessments can be a vital component of a data-informed classroom strategy.

One of the key principles discussed in Chapter 3 is the necessity to align the specific assessment strategy with the learning goals (KUDs). This is perhaps even more critical at the summative assessment phase of student performance because of the decisions tied to those evaluations (e.g., student grades). Furthermore, the interpretations that are drawn from summative assessment data are only as valid as the match between the intended learning goals and the assessment strategy used. Some assessment strategies, such as multiple-choice items, lend themselves to capturing students' recall of factual information such as names, dates, locations, events, the steps in a process, and the meaning of key vocabulary. This factual type of information is necessary, but it is usually insufficient to capture the degree to which students understand the more nuanced aspects of the content within a full unit of study. For that reason, "Big S" summative assessment that more wholly captures the larger profile of student achievement requires that teachers identify and plan for ways that students can more fully demonstrate their developing expertise—generally as a performance.

What Is Performance Assessment?

A performance assessment requires students to apply their knowledge, skills, and understandings in ways detailed in the performance task directions (often called the prompt) and should integrate the KUDs in ways that seem authentic and genuine to them as students. In addition to the clear prompts, students should have access to clear expectations for the performance. Performance assessments typically incorporate clear descriptions of the graduated levels of performance on a rubic aligned to the KUDs and are available to the student in advance of embarking upon the performance assessment to guide their preparation for the assessment as well as their work on the assessment.

Performance assessments have several defining characteristics:

- Provide context and contextual cues that allow students to demonstrate their level of obtainment of clearly defined learning goals.
- Do not seek or allow one-right answer.
- Are connected to real life—that is, transferable outside of the four walls of school, something that Palmer et al. (2008) calls figurative context.
- Can be cross-disciplinary, interdisciplinary, or single disciplinary.
- Require students to engage in 21st-century skills (e.g., problem solving, critical thinking, decision-making, reasoning and thinking).
- Facilitate alignment between the prompt and the accompanying rubric to assess where students are relative to the identified learning goals.
- Can be differentiated in terms of content, process, or product, *although the learning goals remain the same.*

Asking students to demonstrate authentic performances of their knowledge, understandings and skills is well aligned with the philosophy of differentiation. In addition, teachers can hold a common set of expectations for all students and then adjust some of the conditions of the task, such as task complexity, time for task completion, mode of expression, or a student needs to access the task or effectively demonstrate what they know, understand, and are able to do. This feature is consistent with a key principle of high quality differentiated assessment—that is, an effective assessment maximizes the opportunity for a learner to review what he or she knows, understands, and can do. Such supports might include actions such as enabling a student with attention difficulties to work on the assessment over several brief sessions rather than one long session, allowing a student who is new to the English language to write responses in the student's first language with translation assistance to follow, or enabling students to use annotated drawings to express learning rather than requiring only long passages of prose.

Approaching assessment with the common, high expectations for students with provisions for supports as needed reflects the principle of "teaching up" as described in Chapter 1. Thinking about assessment more as a process and less as an "event" also aligns with differentiation philosophy. That is, the teacher engages the students throughout the learning cycle, making them aware of the expectations for the performance assessment as they introduce the unit. Imagine that a teacher introduces a new unit of study in social studies that includes studies of landforms and regions of the United States, as well as critical lessons in utilizing technologies such as maps and GPS software. In the earliest lessons of the unit she may foreshadow what they will be able to do at the end of the unit by describing the eventual performance task: "Students, at the end of this unit, you will be able to demonstrate your understanding of the relationship between economics and geography within the regions of the country by designing a plan for travels that meet specific conditions." Lessons throughout the unit may then refer to the upcoming performance assessment and rubric.

Differentiating Summative Assessments

Because of the role that summative assessments plays in the overall grade a student is given for a unit of study, it is important to understand under what circumstances classroom summative assessments can, and cannot, be differentiated. Recall from Chapter 1, the avenues through which assessments may be differentiated are through the content that makes up the assessment, the process whereby students engage with the assessment, and/ or the product that students create in response to the assessment requirements. In the case of objective classroom summative assessments (e.g., multiple-choice questions, true/false questions, matching questions, fill-in-the-blank), the process of differentiation may occur only through the ways in which students access and respond to the questions but the questions themselves remain the same. For example, with a 50-item multiple-choice and fill-in-the-blank exam, students would respond to the same questions but might access the questions through both audio (i.e., tape-recording of each question) and paper-and-pencil formats; students for whom writing was problematic might respond orally (in person or audio) to fill-in-the-blank questions, thus removing the barrier that would prevent them from fully demonstrating their knowledge, skills, and understandings that the questions were targeting; for students who are easily distracted, the 50 items can be divided into sets (e.g., five sets of ten items); for students with test anxiety, a quiet room without distractors can be provided. In all of these examples, the content remains the same only the process through which students complete the assessment is differentiated.

Again, recalling from Chapter 1, classroom performance assessments can be differentiated through the process of differentiating the content, although the learning targets remain the same, differentiating the process that students engage with the assessment requirements (e.g., use of graphic organizers or check sheets for some students who need organizational support), and/or the product that is produced as a result of responding to the assessment requirements. The following section provides several examples of the ways in which performance assessments may be differentiated and how the resulting data would be used for instructional decision-making.

Planning for and Implementing the Differentiated Performance Assessment

As indicated earlier, if the learning goals are such that students are required to perform (e.g., design and carry out scientific experiments; build a model; create an essay requiring the integration and application of information; or make oral presentations), then the implementation of a performance assessment in all likelihood is appropriate and aligned to the learning goals.

The following scenario describes some of the ways that a teacher might use data prior to administering a differentiated performance assessment, in order to determine which prompt students receive:

Three days before Ms. Calderón, a 6th grade social studies teacher gives her unit's final differentiated performance assessment, she does "Laundry Day" to give students the opportunity to re-visit any content where students feel may benefit from additional work. This will give her additional insights about which differentiated prompt each student will receive. The unit focused on developing students' abilities to effectively read, analyze, synthesize, and use geographic materials (e.g., maps, charts) for specific purposes. The students also studied budgeting in an economics unit earlier in the year but she suspects that students may find it useful to refresh concepts related to budgeting. Students work in self-selected learning centers, each of which focuses on different aspects of the unit. Students turn in their work for Ms. Calderón's review. What she sees will help her determine which prompt each student will receive for the summative assessment. The specific learning objectives for the unit that will be measured in the summative assessment are presented in Table 4.1.

The differentiated performance assessment that Ms. Calderón will give her students as a "Big S" summative assessment has three levels of prompts (see Tables 4.2–4.5). The differentiated performance assessment, *Ultimate Vacation*, is situated within a context that involves planning a trip—a context she has chosen to connect to her students' lives and experiences. Successful responses to the prompt require each student to engage in decision-making and problem-solving skills; every student's response will be evaluated by a rubric (Table 4.6) based on the targeted learning goals. The student work that Ms. Calderón collects from the centers on "Laundry Day" contributes to her decisions about which of the three prompts she gives each student.

All three levels of the performance assessment prompts focus on the pre-identified KUDs; however, they vary in terms of the conditions under which the students will demonstrate their knowledge, understanding, and skills. Because the three

Table 4.1 KUDs for 6th Grade Social Studies Unit

Unit: 6th grade geography (3rd period)
KUDs to be assessed in the performance assessment:
K: Vocabulary (e.g., latitude, longitude, compass, compass rose, economic development, tourism, landforms, human geography, budget, various types of tables and graphs (e.g., bar chart, line graph))

U: Projecting expenses for travel must balance a number of competing priorities and demands. Every decision causes resulting effects.

D: Read and interpret geographic maps
- Organize geographic information by preparing maps, charts, and other graphic displays;
- Analyze and synthesize information about geography using a variety of resources (e.g., maps, texts, reference materials);
- Present data and conclusion in written format using text, tables, and/or graphs; and
- Prepare a detailed and accurate budget.

What's the Purpose of the "Laundry Day" Work: to inform teacher assignment of differentiated tasks for the summative assessment

Table 4.2 Differentiated Performance Assessment: Prompt 1

You and your family are wanting to go on an adventure when school is out this summer. Your family came up with a list of destinations that everyone would like to visit. Your task is to plan *a road trip* for your family of four (two adults and two kids under 13) who want to visit an interesting destination for the family vacation. Your Mom and Dad will tell you maximum distance they wish to travel and how much money the family has budgeted for the trip. You will have access to resources such as maps, tour guides, brochures, the Internet, etc. Use the attached graphic organizer to help you do the following:

1. Calculate the mileage on available routes from your town. Identify the most direct route (the shortest distance in miles to the destination). This is the route your family prefers to travel so that you spend the most time possible at the destination.
2. Calculate the approximate cost of gas for the trip. (Assume their car gets 30 miles to the gallon and gas costs an average of $2.12/gallon.)
3. Your family plans to average 50 miles per hour while driving and travel 6 hours a day. How long will it take you to get to their destination?

Table 4.2 (continued)

---

4. How many nights will you need to spend in hotels on the way to and from your destination? If you stay 4 nights at your destination what will the total cost be for hotels? (Assume that a hotel room costs an average of $75 per night and that your family will stay in one room.)

5. Your family will eat three meals a day. Budget $75 per day. Calculate total meal cost for the complete trip.

6. Once at the destination, your family will need recommendations on what to do. Your family's entertainment budget is approximately $100/day. Make recommendations on the best way to spend this money. Be sure you balance the entertainment and activity needs of both your Mom and Dad and children of the family!

7. Total the cost of travel to the destination, the 4-day stay at the destination, and the cost of the trip back to your town. (If you wish, you may plan an alternative route for their return trip.) Assume your family will average the same amount of driving time per day on the return trip as on the trip to the destination.

8. Are you within the budget? If not, make whatever changes and/or recommendations you need to be within budget.

Now design a detailed itinerary for your family that explains their options for travel and your best recommendations for their trip. Be sure your itinerary is easy to read and understand. Include budget information and recommendations, as appropriate. Create a map (drawn to scale and including all important map elements) and a set of written directions that tells your Mom and Dad what routes to take, when to turn onto a new route, when and where to stop for the night, etc. from the initial departure to the safe return home.

BONUS: Include with your itinerary both an itemized estimate and a detailed explanation of additional expenses that the family may incur on this vacation in order to help them plan more completely and accurately.

You will be evaluated on your ability to advise the family appropriately, the quality of the maps and itinerary you prepare, and the accuracy of your budget. See the attached rubric for more complete information.

Funding for the development of this task was supported under the Educational Research and Development Centers, PR/Award Number R206R50001, as administered by the Office of Educational Research and Improvement, U.S. Department of Education.

Table 4.3 Organizer for Prompt 1

DESTINATION: _____	BUDGET: _____

1. Mileage (Star the most direct route):
   - Route 1: _____
   - Route 2: _____
   - Route 3: _____

2. Cost of Gas:

One way × 2 (roundtrip)	= _____ miles
÷ 30 mpg	= _____ gallons
× \$2.12/gallon	= _____ (Total cost of gas for trip)

3. Total miles one way = _____ miles

÷ 50 mph	= _____ hours
÷ 6 hours/day	= _____ days (total days to destination)

4. Cost of Hotel

Days of travel	= _____ days
× \$75/night	= _____
× 2 (roundtrip)	= _____
+ \$300 (4 days at destination @ \$75/night)	= _____ Total Hotel Cost

5. Cost of Meals

Total days away from home	= _____ days
× \$75/day	= _____ Total Meal Cost

6. Entertainment

Total days at destination	= _____4___ days
× \$100/day	= _____ Total Entertainment Cost

   ADD UP SHADED AMOUNTS:

   GRAND TOTAL COST OF TRIP: _____

prompts measure the same learning goals, the same rubric is used for all students. In Prompt 1, students will find the most explicit set of directions and the task includes a companion graphic organizer to guide each step in the problem solving.

Table 4.4 Differentiated Performance Assessment: Prompt 2

You and your family are wanting to go on an adventure when school is out this summer. Your family came up with a list of destinations that everyone would like to visit. Your task is to plan *a road trip* for your family of four (two adults and two kids under 13) who want to visit an interesting destination for the family vacation. Your Mom and Dad will tell you maximum distance they wish to travel and how much money the family has budgeted for the trip. You will have access to resources such as maps, tour guides, brochures, the Internet, etc. Use the attached graphic organizer to help you do the following:

1. Calculate the mileage on available routes from your town. Identify the most direct route (the shortest distance in miles to the destination). This is the route your family prefers to travel so that you spend the most time possible at the destination.
2. Calculate the approximate cost of gas for the trip. (Assume their car gets 30 miles to the gallon and gas costs an average of $2.12/gallon.)
3. Your family plans to average 50 miles per hour while driving and travel 6 hours a day, stopping twice to each for an hour each time. How long will it take you to get to their destination?
4. Your family will eat three meals a day. Make a recommendation about how much, on average, to budget for each meal. Justify your decision. Calculate the approximate total meal cost for the trip.
5. Your family will stay 4 nights at the destination. Calculate hotel and meal costs for a 4-night stay.
6. Once at the destination, your family will need recommendations on what to do. Your family's entertainment budget is approximately $100/day. Make recommendations on the best way to spend this money. Be sure you balance the entertainment and activity needs of both your Mom and Dad and children of the family!
7. Total the cost of travel to the destination, the 4-day stay at the destination, and the cost of the trip back to your town. (Please plan an alternative route for the return trip.) Assume your family will average the same amount of driving time per day on the return trip as on the trip to the destination.
8. Are you within the budget? If not, make whatever changes and/or recommendations you need to be within budget.

Table 4.4 (continued)

You will also need a detailed itinerary for your family that explains the options for travel and your best recommendations for their trip. Be sure your itinerary is easy to read and understand. Include budget information and recommendations, as appropriate. Create a map (drawn to scale and including all important map elements) and a set of written directions that tells your Mom and Dad what routes to take, when to turn onto a new route, when and where to stop for the night, etc. from the initial departure to the safe return home.

BONUS: Include with your itinerary both an itemized estimate and a detailed explanation of additional expenses that the family may incur on this vacation in order to help them plan more completely and accurately.

You will be evaluated on your ability to advise the family appropriately, the quality of the maps and itinerary you prepare, and the accuracy of your budget. See the attached rubric for more complete information.

Table 4.5 Differentiated Performance Assessment: Prompt 3

The Ultimate Vacation[a]
The AAA Travel Agency in your town is extremely shorthanded and needs additional staff to help travelers plan their vacations for next summer. A list of destinations has been created. You will be assigned a favorite client of the agency, a family of four (two adults and two children under 12). The family has just purchased a brand new mini-van that they plan to take on vacation this summer. Your task will be to suggest an interesting road trip for them to take during this vacation. You will be told how much money the family has budgeted for their trip. You are eager to present them with an interesting and highly appealing trip. You will have access to resources such as maps, tour guides, and brochures, the Internet, etc.
Your task is to do the following:

1. Choose a destination within a reasonable driving distance from your town. Calculate the mileage on available routes. Identify the most direct route. This is the route the family usually prefers to travel so that they spend the most time possible at their destination.
2. Calculate the approximate cost of gas for the trip. Justify your estimate.

Table 4.5 (continued)

---

3. The family prefers to average 50 miles per hour while driving, travel 6 hours a day stopping twice to eat for an hour each time. How long will it take them to get to the destination? How many nights will they need to spend in hotels on the way? Check guidebooks for a hotel that has at least a 2-diamond rating. They prefer hotels that include breakfast. The family usually stays in one room when they travel. Compute hotel costs for each stopover.

4. The family eats three meals a day. Calculate average total meal costs for each trip. Suggest a specific restaurant (or type or restaurant, such as Shoney's, etc.) for each meal. The family generally eats at fast food or family-style restaurants, but they like to splurge on one fancy dinner per trip. You will need to make a recommendation for when and where to enjoy this dinner.

5. The family prefers to stay at least 4 nights at their destination. Calculate hotel and meal costs for a 4-night stay.

6. Once at the destination, the family will need recommendations on what to do. The family's entertainment budget is approximately $100/day. How can they best spend this money? Be sure you balance the entertainment and activity needs of both the adults and children of the family!

7. Suggest at least 1-day trip. (They must be able to drive to the site, see what they want to see, and return to the hotel in the evening.) Plan a trip that is likely to be interesting to both adults and children.

8. The family prefers to take a different route home from their trip.

9. Total the cost of travel to the destination, the 4-day stay at the destination, and the cost of the trip back to your town. Are you within the budget you were given? If not, make whatever changes and/or recommendations needed in order to be within budget.

Now design a detailed itinerary for the family that explains their options for travel and your best recommendations for their trip. Be sure your itinerary is easy to read and understand, since it will be mailed to the family. Include budget information and recommendations, as appropriate. Create a map (drawn to scale and including all important map elements) and a set of written directions that tells the family what routes to take, when to turn onto a new route, when and where to stop for the night, etc. from initial departure to safe return home.

Table 4.5 (continued)

BONUS: *Include with your itinerary both an itemized estimate and a detailed explanation of additional expenses that the family may incur on this vacation in order to help them plan more completely and accurately.*

You will be evaluated on your ability to advise the family appropriately, the quality of the maps and itinerary you prepare, and the accuracy of your budget. See the attached rubric for more complete information.

---

a Funding for the development of this task was supported under the Educational Research and Development Centers, PR/Award Number R206R50001, as administered by the Office of Educational Research and Improvement, U.S. Department of Education.

Table 4.6 Differentiated Performance Assessment Rubric

The Ultimate Vacation Rubric[a]

Still in Training	*Travel Agent*	*World Class Planner*
Budget		
Little or no evidence of logic is applied to the analysis and development of your budget. Mathematical calculations and/ or estimations are incorrect, making your budget plan unusable.	You use logic to analyze and solve budget problems. Appropriate mathematical strategies are chosen, resulting in accurate calculations and/or estimations.	Budget problems are analyzed and solved using logic. Appropriate mathematical strategies are chosen which enable you to accurately calculate or estimate needed figures. The travel budget is not only consistent; it allows room for unexpected or emergency needs.

Table 4.6 (continued)

Still in Training	*Travel Agent*	*World Class Planner*
Planning		
Your planning contains little or no structure. The travel plans fail to follow a logical sequence. You do not consider important aspects of the trip in your plan. Your recommendations for sightseeing and/ or other activities are not appropriate for a family vacation. This trip will be a disappointment to both adults and children.	Your planning is structured. The travel plans follow a logical sequence. You provide sound advice for major aspects of the trip. Recommendations are appropriate, although they tend to favor either the adult OR child perspective. Overall, this trip will be a success.	Your planning is well structured and easy to follow. The travel plans are complete and logical. Your advice to the family is unique and inspired. Recommendations are highly appropriate for all family members, offering a good balance between activities that are likely to please adults and /or children. This trip will be the vacation of a lifetime!
Documents		
Overall presentation is messy and hard to understand. Your map is not drawn to scale and does not include important elements. Travel routes are not clearly labeled and mileage is missing. Accompanying materials such as charts and/or graphs are illegible or not clearly related to itinerary.	Overall presentation is neat and easy to understand. Your map is drawn to scale and includes major elements. Travel routes are labeled, but hard to locate. Mileage is indicated, but in an inconsistent manner. Accompanying materials such as charts and/or graphs are easy to read and relate the itinerary.	Overall presentation is neat and exciting. Your map is drawn to scale, and includes all appropriate elements. Travel routes are clearly labeled and mileage is indicated. Accompanying materials such as charts and/or graphs are professional looking and greatly enhance and/or explain itinerary.

Table 4.6 (continued)

Still in Training	Travel Agent	World Class Planner
Mechanics		
Information is haphazardly organized. Sentences are not supported by details. Word usage is repetitive rather than varied. Errors in spelling, punctuation, and grammar make the itinerary difficult to follow.	Information is organized. Sentences are supported by details and use a variety of words and phrases. Minor errors in spelling, punctuation, and grammar do not interfere with the message.	Information is clearly and succinctly organized. Each sentence is supported by rich and coherent relevant details. Sentences are highly descriptive and make use of a wide variety of words and phrases. Spelling punctuation and grammar are correct.
Bonus (Optional)		
Not applicable	You include with your itinerary an itemized estimate of additional costs that family might incur on the vacation.	You include with your itinerary both an itemized estimate and a detailed explanation of additional costs that the family might incur on the vacation.

a Funding for the development of this task was supported under the Educational Research and Development Centers, PR/Award Number R206R50001, as administered by the Office of Educational Research and Improvement, U.S. Department of Education.

What differentiates Prompt 1 from the others is that it embodies the most structure (i.e., process differentiation). Based upon Ms. Calderón's formative assessments during the unit, as well as her analysis of work from "laundry day," she assigns students to specific tasks. Prompt 1 is given to students who need more support with writing skills, geography and math, and/or who need additional structural support (e.g., organizational aids). In contrast, in Prompt 3, the least structured, students find more complex requirements needed for the travel plan as well as less guidance about how to proceed to planning and budgeting for those conditions. Students completing Prompt 3 will have to carefully analyze the requirements and consider implications when responding to the task. Ms. Calderón assigns Prompt 3 to the students who are working above grade level in reading comprehension, writing, geography and math, and to those students whose data profile suggests they can handle a greater degree of ambiguity. Between the two, Prompt 2 has some degree structure and many opportunities for students to make informed choices when developing their travel plans and budget. Ms. Calderón assigns this prompt to students who are on grade level regarding writing, geography and math skills, and in the cases where data suggest that abundant structure is not necessary. In addition, because the prompts are all based on the same learning objectives, as students are working on the performance task if she discovers that a student working on Prompt 2 or 3 is struggling, Ms. Calderón can easily adjust by modifying the conditions or shifting students to another prompt than the one with which the student began (e.g., a student working on Prompt 3 can be shifted Prompt 2).

Tables 4.7–4.13 highlight an example of a middle school differentiated performance assessment based on content differentiation. In this assessment, students are gathering data from their peers to determine the current market for shoe wear through an in-depth analysis of student preferences. Prompt 1 is targeted to students functioning at grade level in mathematical concepts and processes, and Prompt 2 is for students who are functioning above grade level in both mathematical concepts and abstract thinking. Prompt 2 also has less structure in choosing the characteristics to consider in carrying out the research process. Because of these differences, the rubrics for each prompt are similar but not identical, yet both are aligned with the identified learning goals.

While the learning targets remain the same, Prompts 1 and 2 differ in the type of sampling processes that the students will engage in when collecting data from their peers. Prompt 1 requires simply convenience sampling of their grade-level peers, while Prompt 2 requires students to draw a representative sample of their grade-level peers through either simple random sampling or stratified random

Table 4.7 Consumer Science Learning Targets

Consumer Science
The task and rubric are designed to assess students' ability to collect data, to calculate fractions, decimals, and percentages based on data and to display and report data in graphical and written form through a marketing analysis project.

Learning Targets
- Students will demonstrate their ability to sample a particular population.
- Students will demonstrate their ability to gather information by asking relevant questions (through interviews).
- Students will demonstrate their ability to convert raw data to meaningful data through the use of fractional and decimal manipulations.
- Students will demonstrate their ability to organize information in an effective, concise, and clear manner.
- Students will demonstrate their ability to represent data graphically.
- Students will demonstrate their ability to report data in narrative form.
- Students will demonstrate their ability to communicate findings to a specific audience.

Mathematics, Statistics
- Identify representations of a given percentage and describe the equivalence relationship between fractions and percentages.
- Collect, analyze, display, and interpret data in a variety of graphical methods.
- Solve multi-step consumer application problems involving fractions, and present data and conclusions in graphs, tables, or paragraphs.
- Make inferences based on the analysis of a set of data.
- Use information displayed in graphs and histograms to make comparisons, predictions, and inferences.
- Solve practical problems involving rational numbers and percentages.

Writing
- Write descriptions and explanations
- Develop technical writing

---

a Funding for the development of this task was supported under the Educational Research and Development Centers, PR/Award Number R206R50001, as administered by the Office of Educational Research and Improvement, U.S. Department of Education.

Table 4.8 Rubric for Middle School Math Differentiated Performance Assessment: Prompt 1

Prompt 1	Marketing Wizard	Good Advisor	Missing the Market	Incomplete
Data Collection 1. Questions 2. Sample	1. You develop a set of clear, concise, and specific survey questions that you use consistently for each member in your sample. Your questions address gender, age, shoe preferences, and reasons for preferences in a neutral and unbiased manner. 2. You choose a sample that allows for an accurate and complete representation of your school population.	1. You develop a set of questions that address age, gender, shoe preferences, and reasons for those preferences in a way that allows you to collect data efficiently. 2. You choose a sample that is representative of your school population.	1. You develop a set of questions, but the questions ask for too much information or not enough information. 2. Your sample represents only a part of your school population.	1. You fail to collect data using an established set of survey questions OR your questions do not allow you to gather the kind of information you need to gather for the marketing firm. 2. Your sample does not represent your school population.

Data Reporting				
1. Tables	Your tables contain relevant categories of shoes and reasons for preference. Data is labeled clearly and neatly, enabling the reader to immediately locate data by gender, age, or reason for preference.	Your tables contain relevant categories of shoes and reasons for preference. Although your data categories are inefficient or cumbersome, the reader gets a sense of general preferences. With effort, readers can locate data they are interested in by using table labels.	You provide categories of shoes and reasons for preference in your table, but these categories do not represent the most practical and efficient division of shoe types and reasons for preference. Your table is messy and difficult to follow. Data is presented in a random fashion. It is very difficult to locate data for a particular variable.	You do not use a data table OR your data table does not include all categories of data required. You do not appropriately label the table. Reader cannot locate the data for a particular variable.
2. Thoroughness of Analysis	You analyze all data collected from your sample based on gender, age, or reason for preference.	You analyze all data collected from your sample based on gender, age, and reasons for preference.	You analyze all data collected from your sample based on gender, age, and reasons for preference.	You fail to analyze all data from your sample based on reason for preference.
3. Accuracy of Calculations	Your data calculations are accurate. Your conversions among fractions, decimals, and percentages are correct.	Your calculations are accurate, but you make minor mistakes in your conversions.	Your calculations contain minor errors, which distort your results.	Your calculations contain major errors that affect the accuracy of your conclusions.

Table 4.8 (continued)

Prompt 1	Marketing Wizard	Good Advisor	Missing the Market	Incomplete
Data Reporting 1. Tables/Graphs 2. Report 3. Recommendations	1. You use the most effective tables, charts, and/or graphs to visually display the data so that it is appealing and useful to readers. Your graphs clearly convey the information found in the table. Graphs are labeled and the scale is even and consistent. 2. Your report is direct, concise, and focuses on the results of the data analysis. You state your research questions and the purpose of your research early on in the report. You clearly specify the interview protocol, the sample,	1. You use tables, charts, or graphs to display the data, but another kind of chart or graph might have been more appealing or useful to the reader. Your graphs convey the information found in your table. They are labeled appropriately, but lack precision in scale or data recording. 2. Your report focuses on the results of the data analysis. You state your research questions and explain how you collected data.	1. Inappropriate graphs or charts are used. Omissions or errors in graphs and tables limit the usefulness of the report. Your graphs are difficult to interpret due to errors in mechanics, scale, and precision. 2. Your report relies on opinion more than actual data analysis. The reader is uncertain about some of the details of your data collection, sample, research questions and/or analysis. There are errors in spelling, grammar, punctuation, and/or	1. Your report does not include tables and/or graphs. Your graphs are illegible OR don't represent the data you collected. Tables are not labeled. 2. Your report is ambiguous and opinionated OR you do not provide a report. Mistakes in grammar, spelling, punctuation, and capitalization make it difficult or impossible to read.

how it was collected, and the analysis procedure used. Your report is free of errors in grammar, spelling, capitalization, and punctuation. 3. Your recommendations follow logically from the data you collected. You support your recommendations with a few succinct statements that summarize what you found and make a strong case for your recommendations.	Although you leave out minor details about the interview protocol, sample, collection of data, and/or analysis, these omissions do not obscure the overall validity of the report. You make minor errors in grammar, spelling, capitalization, and punctuation, but they do not interfere with the understanding of the report. 3. Recommendations are logical and are linked to the data presented.	capitalization causing the report to appear unprofessional. 3. You make recommendations, but these recommendations are not related to the data presented in the report OR are not supported by this data.	3. You fail to make recommendations.

Table 4.9 Data Collection Sheet for Differentiated Performance Assessment: Prompt 1

	ID #	Age	Sex	Type of Shoe Preferred									Reason					
				A	B	C	D	E	F	G	H	Other (List)	V	W	X	Y	Z	Other (List)
Shoe Type Code: A_____																		
B_____																		
C_____																		
D_____																		
E_____																		
F_____																		
G_____																		
H_____ Other:																		
Reason Code: V_____																		
W_____																		
X_____																		
Y_____																		
Z_____																		
Other:																		

sampling techniques. Also associated with Prompt 1 are data tables that provide more structure and organization. However, the data tables are not isolated to using with Prompt 1 only. Often, students who are able to engage with complex ideas can also be assisted by organizational structures such as those for Prompt 1.

Table 4.10 Data Analysis Sheet #1 for Differentiated Mathematics Performance Assessment: Prompt 1

Data Analysis Sheet #1								
Type of Shoe Preference	Total # of Students	# of Boys	# of Girls	# of Students Age 10	# of Students Age 11	# of Students Age 12	# of Students Age 13	# of Students Age 14

Table 4.11 Data Analysis Sheet #2 for Differentiated Mathematics Performance Assessment: Prompt 1

Data Analysis Sheet #2

Reason for Choice	Total # of Students	# of Boys	# of Girls	# of Students Age 10	# of Students Age 11	# of Students Age 12	# of Students Age 13	# of Students Age 14

Table 4.12 Differentiated Mathematics Performance Assessment: Prompt 2

Your team is part of Marketing Measurement, Inc., a marketing research company. A local shoe and clothing company, located near your school, recently hired your firm to help them determine what kinds of shoes they should order now for their retail store in order to be stocked for their annual sale **one year from now**. Your team must design, organize, and conduct a research study to help the company make this important decision.

Please follow the steps below to complete your Marketing Management, Inc. assignment. You will be collecting and analyzing data about students and staff's shoe preferences and their likely future buying needs or habits.

Research Preparation:

- Brainstorm ways to gather information about the shoe preferences of kids and staff at your school. You need to gather information about the styles and brands of shoes people have purchased *in the past* as well as those that they think they might buy in the future. The store also wants to know the relative popularity among students and adults of features such as high/low heels, colors, dress/casual, etc.
- You want your results to reflect an accurate and complete picture **of the entire grade level**. You will need to do some research on sample size and selection.
- Decide how many people you should interview and what criteria you should use to choose them (ages, classes, gender, occupation, etc.). Explain your choices.
- Devise a way to measure and record the results of your investigation. Create appropriate tables in which to record your data. Your table must display all the data you collect in a clear and concise format.

Data Collection:

- Conduct your interviews. *It is important to be as consistent as possible in questioning your sample. Be sure to record each subject's gender and age range.*

Data Analysis:

- Analyze your results according to those variables that would most help your clients make decisions about the type of shoes to stock, one year from now. *Justify your decisions.*
- Provide fractions, decimals, and percentages for each variable.

Table 4.12 (continued)

- Convert your results to those types of graphs that would best illustrate the results of your investigation. The information contained in the graphs should be immediately and clearly apparent to the reader.
- Prepare a report for the retail store that hired your company. In the report you must make recommendations about the types of shoes the store should stock to attract students and staff at your school. You must describe your sample and its validity, explain your research process, and present your results in a clear and concise manner. Include appropriate tables and graphs. You must turn in your report and *all supporting materials*, including calculations and justification for your survey questions and sampling decisions. Everything should be neat, clear, and easy to follow.

You will be evaluated on your sampling plan, the accuracy and completeness of your calculations, tables, and graphs, the appropriateness of your recommendations, and the clarity and appeal of your report. Examine the attached rubric for specifics.

In all of the differentiated performance assessment examples provided the question of which prompt should each student receive must be addressed. Since the learning goals for all of the examples are the same, the prompts that each student is given is based upon the evidence collected by the administered of the on-going assessments throughout the unit, as described in Chapter 3. Therefore, it is important that requirements of the performance assessment are considered so that appropriate data can be gathered to facilitate the decision-making regarding assignment of prompts to students. These types of assessments are given, in the majority of circumstances, as a summative assessment at the end of a unit of study, and it is likely that the students will be assigned an overall grade for the unit that can be communicated to both the student and their families in a more formal manner. Therefore, it is useful to explore the topic of grading performance assessments, including differentiated performance assessments, a bit further.

Considerations in the Grading Process

One of the most difficult (and often controversial) responsibilities assigned to a teacher is grading student work. This may be even

Table 4.13 Rubric for Middle School Math Differentiated Performance Assessment: Prompt 2

Prompt 2	Marketing Wizard	Good Advisor	Missing the Market	Incomplete
Data collection 1. Variables 2. Questions 3. Sample	1. You choose the most highly relevant variables to investigate. Your clients will have an excellent chance of finding out the information they most need. 2. You develop a set of clear, concise, and specific survey questions that you use consistently for each member in your sample. Your questions address appropriate variables in a neutral and unbiased manner. 3. You choose a sample that allows for an accurate and complete representation of your grade's student and staff populations.	1. You choose important variables to investigate, allowing your clients to receive important information. 2. You develop a set of questions that address appropriate variables in a way that allows you to data efficiently. 3. You choose a sample that is representative of your school's student and staff populations.	1. You choose variables to investigate, but they are not likely to elicit the information your client seeks important information. 2. You develop a set of questions but the set of questions do not address the client's needs. 3. Your sample represents only a part of your grade level's student and staff populations.	1. You choose inappropriate and/or irrelevant variables to investigate. 2. You fail to collect data using an established set of survey questions or your questions do not allow you to gather the kind of information you need to gather for the marketing firm. 3. Your sample is not representative of your grade level's student and staff populations.

Table 4.13 (continued)

Prompt 2	Marketing Wizard	Good Advisor	Missing the Market	Incomplete
Data reporting	1. Your tables contain relevant categories. Data are labeled clearly and neatly, enabling the reader to immediately locate data by gender, age, or reason for preference.	1. Your tables contain relevant categories. Although your data categories are inefficient or cumbersome, the reader can get a sense of general preferences with effort.	1. You provide in your tables categories but they do not represent the most practical and efficient division variables. Your table is messy and difficult to follow. Data are presented in a random fashion. It is very difficult to locate data for a particular variable.	1. You do not use a data table OR your data table does not include all necessary categories of data. You do not appropriately label the table. Reader cannot locate the data for a particular variable.
1. Tables				
2. Thoroughness of Analysis	2. You analyze all data collected from your sample based on the appropriate variables. Your data calculations are accurate. Your conversions among fractions, decimals, and percentages are correct.	2. You analyze all data collected from your sample based on the appropriate variables.	2. You analyze all data collected from your sample based on the appropriate variables.	2. You fail to analyze all data from your sample.
3. Accuracy of Calculations		3. Your calculations are accurate, but you make minor mistakes in your conversions among fractions, decimals, and percentages.	3. Your calculations contain errors, which distort your results.	3. Your calculations contain major errors that affect the accuracy of your results.

Data Reporting				
1. Tables/graphs 2. Report 3. Recommendations	1. You use the most tables, charts, and/or graphs to visually display the data so that it is appealing and useful to readers. Your visuals clearly convey the information found in the tables. Graphs are labeled and the scale is even, consistent, and correct. 2. Your report is direct, concise, and focused on the results of the data analysis. You state your research questions and the purpose of your research early on in the report. You included your interview protocol, provided details on your sample, how it was collected and the analysis procedures used. You report is free of errors in grammar, spelling, capitalization, and punctuations.	1. You use tables, charts, or graphs to display data, but another kind of chart or graph might have been more understandable and useful to the reader. Your graphs convey the information found in your table. Graphs are labeled appropriately, but lack precision in scale or data recording. 2. Your report focuses on the results of the data analysis. You state your research questions and explain how you collected data.	1. Inappropriate graphs or charts are used. Omissions or errors in graphs and tables limit the usefulness of the report. Your graphs are difficult to interpret due to errors in mechanics, scale, and precision. 2. Your report relies on opinion more than actual data analysis. The reader is uncertain about some of the details of your data collection, sample, research questions, and/or analysis. There are errors in spelling, grammar, punctuation, and/or capitalization causing the repot to appear unprofessional.	1. Your report does not include tables and/or graphs. Your graphs are illegible OR do not represent the data you collected. Tables are not labeled. 2. Your report is ambiguous and opinionated OR you do not provide a report. Mistakes in grammar, spelling, punctuation, and capitalization make it difficult or impossible to read.

Table 4.13 (continued)

Prompt 2	Marketing Wizard	Good Advisor	Missing the Market	Incomplete
	3. Your recommendations follow logically from the data analysis. You support your recommendations with succinct statements that summarize what you found and make a strong case for your recommendations.	Although you leave out minor details about the interview protocol, sample, collection of data and/or analysis, these omissions do not hinder the overall validity of your report. You make minor errors in grammar, spelling, capitalization, and punctuation, but they do not interfere with the understanding of the report. 3. Recommendations are logical and are linked to the data presented.	3. You make recommendations, but they are not related to the data presented in the report OR are not supported by the analysis.	3. You fail to make recommendations.

more complex for teachers whose instruction and assessment practices are guided by the philosophy of differentiation. Invariably, the question arises, "*How do I grade this task since the assessment was differentiated?*" Most germane to this discussion is that the reality that issues surrounding grading are not unique to the context of differentiation, but the curriculum-assessment-instruction cycle more broadly, and the procedures used and decisions that should be made throughout that cycle.

If we imagine that the first step of a journey is to decide the destination, then the first step in teaching and learning is to decide where we intend our students to be after a given segment of learning. Introduced in Chapter 1, and discussed in each following chapter, is the necessity of articulating a clear destination in terms of the most important knowledge, enduring principles and critical skills surrounding a topic of study. Being clear about where we are "traveling" facilitates alignment with the pathways we travel to get there. Imagine an app that asks two questions: what is your destination and what is your current location. Answers to these questions yield a variety of routes—highways, country roads, and options to travel between the two. Teachers create an instructional plan to facilitate making the journey toward the learning goals, differentiated at appropriate times based on students' needs, an assessment plan to gather evidence along the way to determine students' progress and to assist in any changes necessary to keep a student moving forward (on-going assessment), and ultimately to document the level of mastery obtained by students (summative assessment). It is only after these processes have occurred that a teacher is ready to communicate information about student status relative to the learning goals—which is the grading process.

Conceptually, a basic premise in measurement is that a student's observed score (X) on an assessment (whether formal or informal) is the sum of two components: the true score (T; error-free) and an error score (E) (see Eq. 4.1). The goal in defensible classroom assessment is to gather data from students in which the error score is minimized so that the student's score represents as closely as possible the student's true score.

$$X = T + E \qquad \text{Eq. 1}$$

There are many ways that error contributes to a student's "score" in a classroom setting. Error can creep into a classroom assessment at various points throughout the development of the assessment, the collection of data from the assessment, and the scoring of the assessment. The following section identifies ways in which error can influence a student' score, and offers suggestions on how to minimize the error when using classroom performance assessments. It should be noted that when developing classroom performance assessments or scoring classroom performance assessments, teacher's professional judgment is inherent is all aspects.

Development Stage of Classroom Performance Assessments

An important consideration for minimizing error when developing classroom performance assessments is to ensure that the assessment actually represents the targeted learning goals. If a performance assessment is too narrow (e.g., does not measure all identified learning goals), fails to measure important identified learning goals, is based on learning goals that were not part of the instruction, or requires knowledge and/or skills extraneous to the assessment's purpose (e.g., undue reading comprehension), there is concern that the assessment has irrelevant aspects that interfere with students' abilities to demonstrate mastery or proficiency of the targeted learning goals. Having unintentional clues within the performance assessment's task/prompt also adds potential error to students' scores, thereby allowing some students to respond correctly or other students to respond incorrectly in ways that are not relevant to the targeted learning goals.

Scoring Classroom Performance Assessments

Several sources of error can impact students' scores when evaluating performance assessments. Error can come from: (1) the lack of clear and understandable criteria whereby there is inconsistency in the interpretation of the criteria when evaluating students' responses; (2) having a large number of domains or criteria within a domain in an analytic rubric increases the potential for scoring error as research has indicated that it is impossible for a scorer (e.g., teacher) to manage a large number of criteria efficiently (Baryla, Shelley, & Trainor, 2012); and (3) the lack of scorer familiarity or experience with using the rubric also can add potential error to students' scores (e.g., Howell, 2014).

A final consideration that can increase error in students' scores is through the decisions you make during the grading process. For example, giving students the benefit of the doubt ("*I know Sally knows that even though she didn't show it here*") or penalizing students for not following exact directions ("*Jonas didn't do it the way I told him to do it even though he got the correct answer*") are ways in which you contribute to the error score. In the first example, you may give Sally the benefit of the doubt and not subtract from her score even though there is no evidence of student understanding, resulting in "positive" error; in the second example, you subtract from Jonas' score because he did not follow directions although he obtained the correct answer, resulting in "negative" error. Of course, following directions is an important skill in school. If we imagine that a grade reflects students' discipline-related learning, then we should separate academic from non-academic factors when calculating a grade. Not following directions may be problematic and should be addressed outside the grading process. Lumping "following directions" together with "accurately solving equations" creates error. The goal for any classroom assessment situation is to gather, to the extent possible, error-free data so that a student's observed score is reflective of their true score (i.e., $X = T + E$).

Three Keys to Defensible Grading

When engaging in student grading of differentiated performance assessment, guiding essential questions should be:

How confident am I that the grade I give to a student is: consistent (e.g., another teacher would give a similar grade OR if the student could re-take the exam without having learned anything new would the scores be similar); fair to each student (e.g., is based only on that student's performance without any undue influences (e.g., teacher bias or that is some aspect of an assessment gets in the way of a student being able to reveal what he or she knows, that it may be appropriate to differentiate the assessment to remove the potential barriers)), and accurately reflects the student's achievement (i.e., what the student truly knows, understands, and is able to do)?

To help ensure that a teacher's grading practices result in a grade reflective of a student's achievement, three keys to good grading should guide the work:

Key 1: Academic grades are based on clearly identified and targeted academic learning goals. Schools typically define students' academic achievements by the level of obtainment (i.e., student performance) in scholastic areas such as reading, mathematics, science, language arts, history, art, physical education, and drama. Student performance, therefore, should be based on clear learning goals, and it is these learning goals that influence the instructional and assessment choices that you make in order to provide students opportunities to master the goals. Having clarity about the learning goals for students also suggests having clarity about what the learning goals on which student grades should be based.

Key 2: Grades reflect a student's "best and final" performance on major learning goals. Grading policies in many school districts require a set number of grades to be assigned to each student for each reporting period. On the one hand, this policy is good in that it ensures that students' grades are based on a number of assessments instead of just one or two. On the other hand, this policy can be problematic if teachers feel compelled to grade work that should not be graded (e.g., formative assessment), or to grade too early in the learning cycle in order to meet the required number of entries. This practice is problematic for other several reasons. First, grading almost everything (essentially *over-grading*) reinforces the student's extrinsic motivation for learning, rather than intrinsic motivation to engage in work for the purpose of learning rather than simply to earn a grade. Second, over-grading ignores the real possibility that students need time, free of judgment and grades, to engage in and interact with new material and to receive feedback on their work in order to develop understandings and skills. By contrast, ensuring that grades reflect a student's best work with key goals reinforces the idea that a student should have the time and opportunity to practice and receive critical feedback about his or her work with the targeted learning goals in order for him or her to improve and ultimately reach the highest level of proficiency possible. This principle also leads to a third principle of good grading practice, which is that grades should be based on data that are reflective of targeted learning goals rather than data that are unrelated to the students' proficiency with the goals.

Key 3: Reporting separates information about academic and non-academic performances. There is much written about the reality that student grades tend to be aggregation of many factors, many of which are non-academic (e.g., Brookhart, 1993; Brookhart et al., 2016; Brookhart & Nitko, 2019; Cross & Frary, 1999). Such non-academic factors may include perceived level of effort, social behavior, compliance with rules, attendance, and student motivation and participation. While these attributes are important in shaping a student's development, reporting of the attributes should take forms separate from academic grades. Academic grades should be reflective of the level of a student's obtainment of the academic learning targets. Although recent research indicates that teachers include of factors they view as important to achievement (e.g., effort, motivation, participation) in with their grading practices (Brookhart et al., 2016), including these non-academic factors in grades distorts the meaning of the grade if it is to be reflective of the level of proficiency achieved regarding the targeted learning goals. This blending of academic and non-academic factors into grades may be done as a way to facilitate classroom management by rewarding students for good conduct or punishing students for misconduct; it may be that the blending is for the purpose of trying to motivate students to participate in class activities or to try hard in completing required assignments. Whatever the reasons for including academic and non-academic factors in grading, the resulting "fuzziness" element in grades can have huge implications for students. For example, research on the incorporation of homework completion into grades suggests that for new immigrant students grades are in large part determined by not only homework completion but also by their English language proficiency and classroom behavior (Bang, Suázrez-Orozco, Pakes, & O'Connor, 2009). In addition, the authors report that students' understanding of course materials held little importance relative to their language proficiency, leaving the authors to conclude that English skills outweighed teacher perceptions of academic skills in determining these students' grades.

Grading Performance Assessments

Rubrics are the scoring tools used in a performance assessment to evaluate students' level of proficiency and often the question arises as to how to translate the rubric scale to a traditional grading scale. It is important to note that some schools are moving from the traditional grading system to a standards-based grading (SBG) system. There are several reasons for this transition: (1) to bring more consistency within a school as well as across schools in the meaning of a grade, with the focus being on students' strengths and areas for improvement; (2) to attempt to separate out the non-academic factors often used in grades; (3) to create an indicator that aligns directly to the learning standards, which instruction predominantly focuses upon; and (4) to be able to capture students' most recent evidence of mastery of the learning targets. Grading later in the learning cycle allows students the opportunity to make mistakes in their learning without being penalized (i.e., negatively affecting their overall grade). When using performance assessments it is important to consider whether you must translate the students' performance on a rubric to a traditional grading system (e.g., A, B, C, etc.) or whether the performance is part of the evidence in a SBG. For a traditional grading system, Table 4.14 displays how that translation from a rubric to a traditional grading system might look. If, however, a SBG system is in place, then the performance from the assessment would serve as one piece of evidence of a student's mastery of the targeted learning goals.

Table 4.14 Example Translation of a Performance Assessment
Rubric to a Traditional Grading Scale

Performance Assessment Rubric (SBG System)	*Traditional Grading System*	
	Percentage	Letter Grade
Exemplary	90–100	A
Proficient	80–89	B
Basic	70–79	C
Below basic	Below 70[a]	D & F

a Many school districts have implemented a policy that students below basic
receive the highest score in the band (e.g., 69).

Consider the stakeholders with an interest in student grades:
students, parents, counselors, other teachers and school offi-
cials, post-secondary institutions, and employers. Each of these
constituents has a vested interest in using grades for some type
of decision-making. For grades to accurately reflect and communicate to a wide stakeholder audience, they should have a
common meaning—that is, they should communicate accurately a student's achievement with given learning goals or at a
particular point in time.

Summary

Throughout this text, we have emphasized the importance of
first identifying clear learning goals for an instructional cycle.
This clarity allows you to effectively and intentionally focus instruction and the students' attention on the learning objectives.
The clarity also provides for tighter connections between the
learning goals and assessments. When data from assessments
are aligned with targeted learning goals, you can make better inferences about what should happen next instructionally for students. This is the case for pre-assessment, on-going assessment,
and summative assessment. Further, the data collected from
summative assessments, of which performance assessment is one
type, also serves multiple purposes when used appropriately.

Although, in most cases, summative assessments are used as the basis for assigning grades reflective of student performance with targeted KUDs, there are other ways in which the data from summative assessments can be used to improve teaching and learning:

1. Summative assessments serve as pre-assessments in a curriculum that is vertically coherent. That is, if a curriculum is organized and sequenced so that student learning continues to build from one unit of study to the next unit of study (i.e., vertically aligned), the summative assessment may serve as a pre-assessment for the upcoming unit.

2. Summative assessments can serve as a guide for a teacher improving his/her instructional methods. Teachers should look at patterns of responses in their class data asking themselves: How well did the class do as a whole? Who were the strong and weak students and what made students' responses "strong" or "weak"? Did students all choose the same wrong answer? Why or why not? Asking these types of questions about student responses, which is a form of feedback for the teacher, allows a teacher to self-reflect on the effectiveness of approaches to teaching and the degree to which the approaches address students' needs. Reflecting on one's teaching practices based on data collected from student assessments often focus on the alignment between the instruction carried out and the assessment given, the actual process of teaching (content presented, resources used, opportunities provided, scaffolding, etc.).

3. Summative assessments can also assist teachers and administrators in curriculum improvement efforts. If summative assessments show consistent gaps between the learning targets and students' knowledge, skills, and understandings, particularly across multiple teachers' classrooms, schools may consider revising the curriculum or creating a new curriculum to fill in learning gaps. This type use of student data differs from the use of formative data discussed in Chapter 3 as it is based on instruction that is "completed," whereas data from formative assessments help guide future instruction.

In general, high-quality summative assessments are an essential component of the curriculum-assessment-instruction cycle that can serve important purposes in addition to communicating students' levels of proficiency with the targeted learning goals. As laid out in this chapter, these types of classroom assessments can also provide information about existing curricular gaps or areas where the content can be extended as well as serve as a source of information for a teacher's self-reflection upon their overall instructional prowess for that particular unit of study and where future changes might be warranted.

References

Baryla, E., Shelley, G., & Trainor, W. (2012). Transforming rubrics using factor analysis. *Practical Assessment, Research and Evaluation, 17*(4), 1–7.

Brookhart, S. M. (1993). Teachers' grading practices: Meaning and values. *Journal of Educational Measurement, 30,* 123–142. doi:10.1111/j.1745-3984.1993.tb01070.x

Brookhart, S. M., Guskey, T. R., Bowers, A. J., McMillan, J. H., Smith, J. K., Smith, L. F., Stevens, M. T., & Welsh, M. E. (2016). A century of grading research: Meaning and value in the most common educational measure. *Review of Educational Research, 86,* 803–848. doi: 10.3102/0034654316672069

Brookhart, S. M., & Nitko, A. J. (2019). *Educational assessment of students* (8th ed.). New York, NY: Pearson.

Cross, L. H., & Frary, R. B. (1999). Hodgepodge grading: Endorsed by students and teachers alike. *Applied Measurement in Education, 12,* 53–72. doi: 10.1207/s15324818ame1201_4

Howell, R. (2014). Grading rubrics: Hoopla or help? *Innovations in Education and Teaching International, 51*(4), 400–410.

Palmer, B. C., Shackleford, V., Miller, S. C., & Leclere, J. T. (2006). Bridging two worlds: Reading comprehension, figurative language instruction, and the English-language learner. *Journal of Adolescent & Adult Literacy, 50,* 258–267.

5

Bringing Differentiated Assessment Data Use Full Circle

The Role of Teacher as Action Researcher

In Chapter 1, we describe the many ways that contemporary classrooms reflect our increasingly diverse nation, making it even more important for teachers to use data generated from differentiated classroom assessments to make learning a good fit for all students. In Chapters 3 and 4, we walked through specific examples that showed how teachers in different subjects and grade levels differentiated formative and summative assessments to meet the needs of their multifaceted students. In this chapter, we take a step back to look at the process from a wider view to see how the pieces fit together and to consider a model of data use practice that could be employed by individual teachers, groups of teachers across a grade level, or an entire school. The purpose of this chapter is to provide a common vocabulary and a common framework that teachers and other stakeholders can use, across different educational settings, for the purposes of utilizing data from differentiated classroom assessments for informed decision-making.

In today's educational settings, using data to plan, monitor, and adjust instruction is an expectation of most public school teachers, whether it be through engagement in a school's professional learning community (PLC), a content- or grade-level data team, engaging with a data coach, or each teacher individually planning. Predominantly, most of the data-use conversation has been around school improvement, focusing on data that are generated by large-scale assessments (e.g., interim benchmarks, accountability testing). The expectation that schools, administrators, and teachers use data is not new; yet, much of the literature around data-use in school settings indicate educators often have difficulties with knowing what to do with the data, despite the wide availability of guidebooks (e.g., Marsh, Pane, & Hamilton, 2006).

Several conceptual frameworks that explore the steps of data use practice are described in the literature and provide a helpful roadmap for differentiated assessment. For example, Coburn and Turner (2011) outline three steps in the data use process: noticing, interpreting, and constructing implications, but they make clear that these processes are situated within a larger organizational and political context. Another framework offered by Mandinach (2012) closely examines what we mean by the very terms surrounding this work. She distinguishes "data" as the raw material (i.e., test scores, student products), which is only made useful when it is translated into interpreted "information" that is rooted specifically within a context. For example, an incorrect response on a specific math problem connects the raw score with the intended learning target. The third component is then the "knowledge" that results from the teacher connecting the interpretation of the "information" into a related plan of instructional action. In other words, seeing the student's pattern of missed math problems connects with the teacher's knowledge of the mathematics content to inform a plan of action that is implemented and the resulting impact examined.

Both the Coburn and Turner (2011) and Mandinach (2012) frameworks share common elements regarding the emphasis on data use, and also examine other factors that influence data use for decision-making (e.g., teacher beliefs; organizational structures;

political contexts). For example, how teachers feel about students can unintentionally influence how they go through the process of analyzing and making meaning from the data—to either the student's advantage or disadvantage. Teachers' decisions are never driven completely by data since they filter the data through their own lenses and experiences (Datnow, Greene, & Gannon-Slater, 2017). Cognitive biases have also been shown to influence decision-making (e.g., West, Toplak, & Stanovich, 2008). These biases are the thinking patterns that teachers may hold based on their observations of students that may lead to inaccurate judgments and faulty logic. These types of biases originate from the phenomenon of seeing what one would expect to see (confirmation bias), or by omitting information that is perceived as risky (omission bias), suggesting that instruction was less than stellar. We may also be biased in decision-making by over-reliance on our prior knowledge about students.

Contextual factors also influence the process of data collection and sense-making. One of these contextual factors is the school's organizational structure. Teachers who have access to technological tools, such as a data dashboard, or to professionals within their school, such as a data coach, have assets that can facilitate the ease of and consistency in the use of data. Another consideration that shapes teachers' data use is the political context in which the work occurs. For example, having a formal policy mandating data use can result in school leaders prioritizing spending for data dashboards and data coaches to ensure that the policy is enacted.

Each teacher is central to the process of data use for instructional decision-making. Using data for decision-making requires not only the individual knowledge and skills related to data use but also analytical and action-oriented tasks (Coburn & Turner, 2011). In the following section we present a process that can be used regardless of the grade level or academic content area by placing the teacher at the center of data use in the role of action researcher. Let's examine how the key ideas form Coburn and Turner (2011) and Mandinach (2012) take shape in a practical context. The teacher takes ownership of her class and in doing so, assumes the role of action researcher.

Teacher as Action Researcher

Imagine this—a high school English teacher notices that a small group of students seem to "tune out" during her first period class, and she commits to figuring out why this is happening so that she can do something to address the problem. She considers that students may be bored or struggling, they may be having self-confidence issues about themselves as learners, or there may be some other personal or academic circumstances that influence their ability to positively engage. Using a variety of methods, she systematically observes the students for a period of several days to note patterns. She keeps notes on classroom conditions when she sees the problem behaviors. She also makes a point to check in with the students' teachers during second period to see if the behaviors occur there as well. Armed with the data she has collected, she organizes what has been gathered, analyzes the data, and combines the results from the various data sources (about the environment, the students, the curriculum, the instructional context). She then uses the information to design instructional actions to address the students' needs.

This process is an integral part of the work of teachers, positioning them within the classroom context as an action researcher. In the role of "teacher as action researcher," teachers reflect systematically on student data from assessments, differentiated or not, with the intent of planning for students' needs. Within a school setting, teacher as action researcher can be one of several configurations: as an individual teacher researcher, as collaborative teachers as researchers (e.g., grade level) group, or as school-wide teachers as researchers group. Regardless of the configuration of the research process (individual, collaborative, or school-wide), each includes the following steps (Figure 5.1).

Step One: Identifying an Area of Interest or Concern

One area that has received attention in the last 10–15 years is *teacher noticing.* Coburn and Turner (2011) consider "noticing"

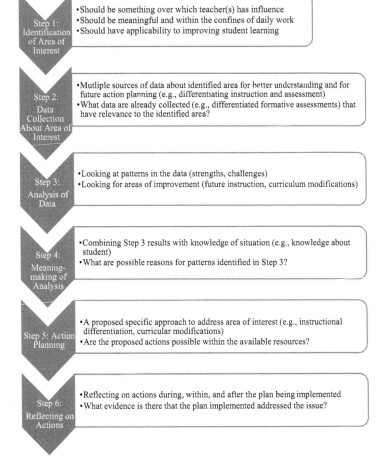

Step 1: Identification of Area of Interest
- Should be something over which teacher(s) has influence
- Should be meaningful and within the confines of daily work
- Should have applicability to improving student learning

Step 2: Data Collection About Area of Interest
- Mutliple sources of data about identified area for better understanding and for future action planning (e.g., differentiating instruction and assessment)
- What data are already collected (e.g., differentiated formative assessments) that have relevance to the identified area?

Step 3: Analysis of Data
- Looking at patterns in the data (strengths, challenges)
- Looking for areas of improvement (future instruction, curriculum modifications)

Step 4: Meaning-making of Analysis
- Combining Step 3 results with knowledge of situation (e.g., knowledge about student)
- What are possible reasons for patterns identified in Step 3?

Step 5: Action Planning
- A proposed specific approach to address area of interest (e.g., instructional differentiation, curricular modifications)
- Are the proposed actions possible within the available resources?

Step 6: Reflecting on Actions
- Reflecting on actions during, within, and after the plan being implemented
- What evidence is there that the plan implemented addressed the issue?

Figure 5.1 Action Research Process

to be the first step in the data use process. Although there is not a common understanding of the term's meaning, at the core of each definition is the idea that you must pay attention to what is occurring in your classroom, and, in some way, respond to what you notice. At times, this response can be in-the-moment, during instruction, and at other times it may be a more deliberate, thought-out, planned response. Rodgers (2002) argues that teachers need the ability "to see student learning: to discern, differentiate, and describe the elements of that learning, to analyze the learning and then respond" (p. 231). We define this practice as the teacher's professional ability or vision to notice things (e.g., events, student engagement or lack thereof, student interactions, classroom talk) in an area that piques the teacher's interest, perhaps because the environment is not optimal for student learning or because the teacher sees an opportunity to optimize an area for even greater potential whether it be for one student, several students, or the whole class (Goodwin, 1994). In this step differentiated assessment occurs to reflect the strengths, weaknesses, and interests of each student.

For the purposes of this text, we have focused primarily on the use of data for instructional improvement, although it is important to note that data may also be used for accountability purposes or for school improvement. Within the area of instructional improvement, noticing means assessment of student learning and considerations of the factors that affect that outcome. Among areas ripe for teachers' attention are:

- Students' engagement: Are all students engaged or are only some of the students engaged in the learning process?
- Students' performance on assessments: Overall, what areas were strong, what areas were weaker? Are there subgroups of students that performed better or worse in all areas or in particular areas?
- Parental engagement: Are parents involved and supporting their child's learning?

Imagine the scenario in which the teacher identifies "student talk" as the area of interest. She sees some students frequently expressing ideas, asking questions, pressing on their peer's ideas and she also sees students who rarely engage in classroom discourse. Some of the more reserved students are non-native English speakers, others are just quiet and less willing to take risks. Identifying this as an area of interest dovetails with differentiated assessment, as we will see in Step 2. This first step in the data use process is identifying an area of interest or concern and is because it serves as the guide for the second step, data collection. Often the data collection process and the data analysis process are referred to a progress-monitoring, and many teachers report they are not as confident in these two processes (Filderman & Toste, 2018).

Step Two: Data Collection

Collecting data as part of a teacher-as-researcher process means: (1) using data that are already collected for another purpose and that are either directly related to the area of interest, and/or (2) engaging in the collection of data that directly relate to the area of interest. In the earlier scenario, the teacher may collect data through multiple approaches to document the frequency of student-initiated responses, to observe students engaged in peer-group tasks; and to interview students one-on-one to listen to their ideas. For another example, consider a teacher who has asked that the parents of her students to check their child's school account once a week for updates on how their child is progressing, what their child is/has been working on, and what will be coming up in the near term. If the teacher notices that the student has not been turning in homework, the teacher can verify that the parent has logged in (i.e., data already collected for another purpose). If the verification indicates that the parent has routinely checked in, then it is reasonable to consider that the parent knows about the homework. The teacher may then consider other types of data needed to address the issue of the student not submitting homework.

A further example of the process of data collection for addressing issues or concerns is using the data from previously administered summative assessments. For instance, as described in Chapter 4, the differentiated performance assessment administered at the end of a unit of study can be used for multiple purposes: (1) to document student learning, (2) to identify areas for future growth for each student, (3) to reflect on the instruction and the learning activities for areas of improvement (i.e., teacher reflection), and/or (4) for curriculum revision.

For the area of using data for curriculum revision purposes, a separate set of questions should be generated to inform decisions about adjustments that might need to be made. The first step in this process is identifying the specific questions that are answerable by the data obtained from the summative assessment. Once the questions have been generated, the process pivots to ask what changes can be made to the curriculum to address the concerns, issues, or patterns revealed in the summative assessment analysis, and how high a priority each potential change might be. As this process unfolds, additional data may need to be gathered before finalizing any curriculum revisions. For example, data from actual classroom resources (e.g., activities) may be required to determine the degree of alignment between the curriculum, the resources, and the assessment. In this instance, data are not just student performance results but also include the actual materials used during instruction.

Step Three: Data Analysis

The process of data analysis is where the data use process becomes iterative. Once the data analysis stage begins we may realize that: (1) additional data need to be collected or (2) more questions need be asked requiring additional data collection. In any case, questions should uncover the needs, priorities, or resources required to address the area of interest/concern. Common themes that might drive the data analysis phase for differentiated assessment include, among others.

Identifying Student Performance Differences

How do student outcomes differ by groups within a class and across classes? Are there specific areas that need improvement for some students, for all students? For example, when looking over the differentiated performance assessment noted in Chapter 4, an 8th grade social studies teacher asked the following questions: Which of my students scored at the "World Class Traveler" level, the "Travel Agent" level, and the "Traveler-in-Training" level? Of the students scoring at each level, are there performance patterns each score level? For each class, a teacher might look at the highest scores and the lowest scores to determine if there are patterns of differences in students' performances: Are the highest scores associated with certain groups of students or certain activities or resources with which the students have engaged? Are the lowest scores associated with certain groups of student or certain individual students? Were there common misunderstandings in the group that perhaps reflect perhaps a breakdown in the instruction at a particular time?

Identifying Areas for Improvement

Using the data for improvement can serve two differentiation purposes: (1) improvement for future instruction within a unit or (2) improvement in curricular documents.

Future Instructional Improvement. What aspects of student performance can be optimized for instructional improvement? Were certain content areas or strategies not emphasized in instruction or over-emphasized? Were particular materials more or less associated with student success or failure? Are there specific areas that could be extended for certain students, or all students?

Curricular Improvement. Are there areas in student performance that suggest curriculum revisions are needed or that there are gaps in the content in the curriculum? Are there different strategies, approaches, or resources that should be included in the curriculum?

Once the essential questions are identified and the data analyzed to address the questions, the next step is to make sense of the results of the analysis—the meaning-making stage. This is also the stage where additional questions may be generated to better help understand the area of interest. When this is the case, the processes of data collection and data analysis continue (i.e., becomes iterative).

Step Four: Meaning-making: Information Generating

The purpose of the meaning-making process is to generate information—to combine the results of the analyses with an understanding of the situation (e.g., climate environment, knowledge about students)—for the purpose of taking actions to address the identified area of interest. In the Chapter 4 example from the differentiated performance assessment, while the data analysis stage gave the teacher a picture of student progress, it did not tell her what, if anything, to do to modify instruction or the curriculum moving forward. As an example, after administering the differentiated performance assessment, the teacher wanted to examine which students consistently scored above and below the targeted performance level. The teacher graphed the data into three groups: (1) those that scored above the target ("World Class Planner"), (2) those that scored below the target ("Traveler-in Training"), and (3) those that scored near or around the target ("Travel Agent"). In reviewing the results and taking into consideration the curriculum, the resources that were used during instruction, and the students' needs, the teacher decides that students who scored in the "World Class Planner" range need additional levels of challenge during the learning cycle. As a result, she examined aspects in her instruction and resources that she could modify to provide extended challenge for advanced learning in future classes. For students in the "Travel Agent" range, because this range indicates success with the targeted goals, she will make no changes, and for students below the targeted range, she will use a different instructional approach and some different resources with continuation of data collection to monitor the students' movement toward the identified learning targets.

Step Five: Action Planning

With information in hand focused on the targeted areas of interest, the next step in the data use process is to plan the action that is needed to address the issue or concern, or in other words, what is needed to implement solutions resulting from the sense-making, information-generating stage.

Let's consider the earlier example using the performance assessment from Ms. Caledrón's class. Ms. Caledrón was making sense of the data from the students' responses on the performance assessment for different purposes in order to take specific actions. First, she summarized each student's level of proficiency related to the targeted learning goals—she used the rubric to assign student grades based on their performance on the assessment. Second, she considered the results of the assessment from a formative stance, analyzing students' achievement on the performance assessment. What she learned from the students' levels of proficiency had implications for the upcoming unit and provided her with insights about how she would differentiate for the students' needs. Third, she used the results from the students' performance assessment responses to analyze the alignment between the curriculum, assessment, and instruction to identify areas in which there were gaps or areas that needed to be enhanced in a future iteration of the curriculum. The area of interest identified for investigation determines the types of responses required. Whether for instructional improvement, addressing specific students' needs through differentiated instruction, or curriculum revising, each purpose requires different types of actions.

Step Six: Reflecting on Actions

Reflection should be on-going throughout each of the steps so that revisions can be made during implementation if necessary, but the final phase of the Teacher as Researcher process is for you to systematically reflect on the degree to which the action plan addressed the identified interest. This stage is where you review what happened, determine if the actions were effective, and make decisions about future steps to be taken.

A Brief Example

Now that we have summarized each of the six steps involved in the action research process, we will consider another example where each step is briefly described. Our example starts with Mr. Templeton, a fifth-grade elementary lead teacher who is reviewing the most recent data from the differentiated common math assessment. He wants the grade-level team (himself, another teacher, and the math specialist) to investigate how to improve student achievement during the next six weeks before the mid-year interim assessment is given.

Step One: Identification of Area of Interest

Mr. Templeton, the lead teacher, Ms. Hurst, the other grade-level teacher, and Ms. Ashby, the math specialist, meet during their weekly planning block to take a closer look into the patterns of achievement across various subgroups. As the teachers discuss the charge, they realize that because the common assessment was differentiated (task differentiated/same rubric), they need to break down the overall assessment results by student groups, by the two prompts, and by each teacher's classroom.

Step Two: Data Collection about Area of Interest

Because the data the teachers were analyzing were from the most recent common formative assessment from the first unit of the year, there were no new data to collect. However, Ms. Ashby, the math specialist, asked each teacher to bring the lesson plans each used to teach the unit so that they could look at each teacher's instructional approach to the unit, trying to identify if there were particular approaches that seemed to better position students for mastering the unit's learning goals.

Step Three: Analysis of Data

Prior to coming to the meeting, Ms. Ashby created two additional tables that broke the overall student performance results down by various student groups (ELL, gender, race/ethnicity) and prompts by each teacher's classroom. Over the course of four weeks, the three teachers "dug into" not only these data but also the lesson plans taught by each teacher. In their analysis of the lesson plans, each teacher described the plans by considering the following questions: *What specific instructional strategies were used in the lessons? How was student learning assessed in each lesson (e.g., on-going, summative)? What were the resources used? Where there particular instructional activities that seemed to allow students to make meaningful connections to the content topics?*

Step Four: Meaning-making of Analysis

As the teachers analyzed the data tables, lesson plans, and the results of the common formative assessment, it was clear that the teachers approached the same unit in very different ways. Mr. Templeton preferred to teach a mini-lesson on the math topic to all students followed by students completing the problem sets in the textbook. When students were finished, they checked their answers with him, and if they were correct they were dismissed to begin their homework or use math problem solving apps on their computers. Ms. Hurst explained how she approached the unit: she organized her unit's KUDs and implemented a pre-assessment. When reviewing the students' responses on the five-item pre-assessment it became clear that students were in very different places relative to the goals of the unit and she quickly realized that she would need to differentiate the mathematics instruction accordingly while still making the entire class a collaborative learning community. Ms. Hurst began each class period with an "entrance ticket" that focused on a key concept or skill and invited students to work with a classmate to solve the problem and show how they came to their answer using models and written explanations. While students worked, she listened to their "math talk" and posed questions to students to prompt their thinking. When it was clear that students' understandings diverged into groups, she had tiered work tasks ready—some with more teacher direction, concrete manipulatives, and computer models; others with extended problem sets with increasing aspects of complexity. As the students engaged in the different lessons, Ms. Hurst indicated that she jotted down notes about each student—which student was still struggling, which student showed increasing understanding of the concepts covered in the lesson, which student showed greater insight into the concepts? Ms. Hurst indicated that her answers to these questions then guided her next set of lesson planning for the unit. In addition, on most days students completed an exit ticket that asked them to self-assess how comfortable they were with the math concepts from the day.

After looking at the data tables and listening to each other discussing their lesson plans, the three teachers came to the conclusion that, because Ms. Hurst had consistently differentiated instruction and assessments throughout the unit, her students performed markedly better on the end-of-unit common assessment.

Step Five: Action Planning

Once the teachers completed their analysis and meaning-making activities, they approached revision of the curriculum unit for next year by incorporating more differentiation strategies to engage all students in the learning at a level that was appropriate for where they are at a particular moment with the target learning goals. The teachers outlined the specific steps that they would take in order to achieve their goal of differentiating the lesson plans within the unit. Some of the changes that they purposed to the unit included:

1. Align the KUDs for the unit with the common formative assessments and ensuring that the unit's lesson goals incorporated the state's math standards.
2. Create learning progressions that provided the team with the key mathematical concepts from the grade levels below/above theirs so that they were ready to reinforce prerequisite concepts or extend into the next level of complexity.
3. Develop a unit pre-assessment aligned to unit goals with the understanding that it would be administered a week prior to the start of the unit. Build-in time to analyze the students' responses increases the likelihood that the data are used to improve instruction. If appropriate, consider ways to differentiate the pre-assessment to ensure that the process of gathering this information did not get in the way of students' sharing what they already know—reducing the "error."

4. Create a range of teaching materials and supplementary texts that allow for more visual displays of the topics and graphic organizers that demonstrated steps in a process. These resources were conceptualized for struggling students but all students could use them.

5. Actively plan for pathways throughout the unit where student groupings would be based on daily formative assessments (e.g., exit tickets, journal prompts, problem sets) as well as more formal assessments ("little s" summative assessments).

6. Ensure that throughout the unit, there are opportunities for students to "do mathematics" where content is presented in multiple ways (e.g., verbally, visually). These opportunities would ask students to take an active role in their own learning (determining students' interests about the topic as well as their own self-assessments) and would incorporate their input into instructional plans.

7. Create a classroom space where students could work quietly without distraction as well as a space where students could collaborate with classmates.

Step Six: Reflecting on Actions

The two teachers and the math specialist debriefed the "teacher as researcher" process by considering several questions: *How well did they believe the process worked? Are there additional data that could be brought into the discussion? Are there specific resources or professional learning opportunities that are needed to carry out the identified unit's revisions and the teaching of the unit next year?* Answering these questions help guide the implementation of the differentiated unit for the next year. In the case of the 5th grade math team, their journey into systematic professional reflection about using differentiated instruction and assessments throughout their unit opened up a new way of teaching for Mr. Templeton and increased the prospect of improved teaching and learning for all of the students in the grade level.

Making Decisions based on High-Quality Data from Differentiated Classroom Assessment

Not surprisingly, poor quality data leads to less effective decision-making. Logically then, teachers and other educators who seek to make instructional or curricular improvements should make every effort to ensure that data on which they base plans on is of high quality. Decisions about teaching and learning can have major consequences for student learning. So what does this mean for differentiated classroom assessments?

It is important to remember that employing good assessment practices is an essential part of effective teaching. To both teach effectively and use good assessment practice requires that teachers, regardless of the assessment type (pre-assessment, formative assessment, summative assessment):

1. Understand how the data from the assessment will be interpreted and used. For instance, being able to specifically answer *why* one is giving a pre-assessment or a final exam helps frame the assessment so that appropriate data can be generated from the assessment. For example, for a pre-assessment you might want to gather evidence of students' interests in order to more fully engage students in the upcoming unit, or you might want to use the pre-assessment data for making grouping decisions based on students' readiness to learn the materials. In either case, you must ensure that you have clarity on the targeted learning goals and any prerequisite knowledge or skills that students will need to have mastered before starting the unit. Again, having clarity about the purpose of the pre-assessment determines the types of questions that are asked and the ways in which the data are subsequently used.
2. Ensure that ongoing differentiated classroom assessments allow students to accurately demonstrate their proficiency with the identified learning targets. That is, a differentiated classroom assessment used in a formative way must allow students to engage in the appropriate level of cognitive

complexity. As teachers we have control over how we approach this and so we can intentionally differentiate the implementation. For example, if the learning target indicates that students can use elements of experimental design when carrying out scientific investigations, it is important that the differentiated assessment provide the opportunity for students to engage in designing a scientific experiment, collecting meaningful data, analyzing the data collected, and presenting the results of the investigation. The differentiated aspect the assessment might include the provision of scaffolds such as data organization charts or prompting questions for students to consider as they are designing their experiment. Doing anything other than a scientific investigation (e.g., writing a project proposal) results in a misalignment between the learning target and the assessment.

3. Ensure that all differentiated assessments minimize the potential for *bias*. Bias in assessment items is the "presence of some characteristics of an item that results in differential performance for individuals of the same ability but from different ethnic, sex, cultural, language, or religious groups" (Hambleton & Rodgers, 1995, p. 1). The biasing of assessment items can occur through from the language used in an assessment item (e.g., use of unfamiliar terms), the context of the item (e.g., lack of certain types of experiences), or in the stereotyping of groups.

4. Relate students' results from differentiated classroom assessments to meaningful descriptions of their knowledge, skills, and understandings. Doing this allows you to continue to incorporate appropriate differentiation aspects to your instruction. For example, giving students a score of 75/100 carries no qualitative meaning to what they know, understand, and can do and gives little insight into the areas where they missed the targets. What it conveys is that the student achieved 75% of some body of information without being specific to where they met expectations and where they fell short. In this example, it is important that teachers are able to clearly translate what the score of 75

means by qualitatively describing what the student knows, understands, and can do. This may be particularly germane when differentiated items are used (varying modality, content, etc.). In this case, 75% for one student reveals a very different picture than 75% for another student. This clarity results in your being able to differentiate your instruction to better suit students' needs. It is also important that the "75" communicate the same in terms of levels of performance regardless of the student. This same issue occurs when we use other representations of performance such as a letter grade.

Because classroom differentiated assessments are typically designed and routinely given by teachers to determine students' proficiency levels of targeted learning goals, the data must be of high-quality. Following the guidelines presented above will go a long way toward gathering differentiated classroom assessment data to ensure accurate and appropriate decisions for instructional planning.

Summary

In this chapter, we have outlined to process whereby you can engage in a systematic way with data to make instructional decisions, whether those decisions are about your instruction on a current unit of study or whether the instruction is about a future unit of study. We hope that it provides a common sense way of incorporating data from differentiated classroom assessments into your instructional decision-making so that you can better address the academic needs of your students.

This book has focused on using data differentiated classroom assessments to drive instructional planning. We hope that you have learned that in order to best support instructional differentiation that the assessments and the assessment process themselves must also be differentiated and that the differentiation of assessment can occur in a variety of ways.

References

Bang, H. J., Suarez-Orozco, C., Pakes, J., & O'Connor, E. (2009). The importance of homework in determining immigrant students' grades in schools in the USA context. *Educational Research, 51*(1), 1–25. DOI: 10.1080/00131880802704624

Coburn, C. E., & Turner, E. O. (2011). Research on data use: A framework and analysis. *Measurement: Interdisciplinary Research and Perspectives, 9*, 173–206.

Datnow, A., Greene, J. C., & Gannon-Slater, N. (2017). Data use for equity: Implications for teaching, leadership, and policy. *Journal of Educational Administration, 55*, 354–360. doi: 10.1108/JEA-04-2017-0040

Filderman, M. J., & Toste, J. R. (2018). Decisions, decisions, decisions: Using data to make instructional decisions for struggling readers. *Teaching Exceptional Children, 50*, 140–130. doi: 10.1177%2F0040059917740701.

Goodwin, C. (1994). Professional vision. *American Anthropologist, 96*, 606–633.

Hambleton, R., & Rodgers, J. H. (1995). Item bias review. *Practical Assessment, Research & Evaluation, 4*(6). Retrieved from https://pareonline.net/getvn.asp?v=4&n=6.

Mandinach, E. (2012). A perfect time for data use: Using data-driven decision-making to inform practice. *Educational Psychologist, 47*, 71–85. doi: 10.1080/00461520.2012.667064

Marsh, J. A., Pane, J. F., & Hamilton, L. S. (2006). *Making sense of data-driven decision making in education: Evidence from recent RAND research.* Retrieved from www.rand.org.

Rodgers, C.R. (2002) Seeing student learning: Teacher change and the role of reflection. *Harvard Educational Review, 72*, 230–253.

West, R. F., Toplak, M. E., & Stanovich, K. E. (2008). Hueristics and biases as measures of critical thinking: Associations with cognitive ability and thinking dispositions. *Journal of Educational Psychology, 100*, 930–941. doi: 10.1037/a0012842

Index

Note: **Bold** page numbers refer to tables; *italic* page numbers refer to figures and page numbers followed by "n" denote endnotes.

Made in the USA
Columbia, SC
05 June 2024

36682102R00074